D0768413

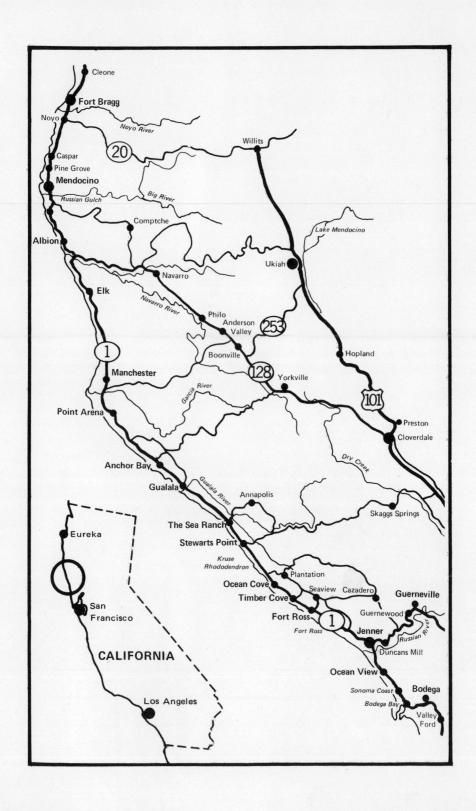

Can You Survive Your Escape?

CAN YOU SURVIVE YOUR ESCAPE?

Life on California's North Coast

Roger Verran

Presidio Press
San Rafael, California • London, England

Library of Congress Cataloging in Publication Data

Verran, Roger, 1916–
    Can you survive your escape?: Life on
California's north coast.

    1. Verran, Roger, 1916–   2. Gualala,
Calif. — Biography.   3. California — De-
scription and travel — 1951–   4. Seaside
resorts — California.   I. Title. F869.G83V47
979.4'15   78-3461
ISBN 0-89141-066-X pbk.

Published by Presidio Press
1114 Irwin Street
San Rafael
California 94901

Cover design by Barbara Ravizza

Drawings by Nick Carter

Printed in the United States of America

For my wife, Shirley,
who started the whole thing

CONTENTS

Line drawings by
NICK CARTER

Photography is, for the most part, by the author, whose technique is to point, shoot and pray. Several photos, however, were contributed by his daughter, Julie, a young pro who has had a number of shows, and by Nick Carter, an old pro and an old friend.

THE INEVITABLE
QUESTION

To pull up stakes and head for the boondocks could well be the new American Dream.

George Gallup, the pollster who tells us what we think, recently reported that nine out of ten Americans would prefer to live in a town, village or some other rural area. Surveys being what they are, I know that people don't always mean precisely what they say.

But a nine out of ten figure is impressive.

If my wife and I had known such an idea would suddenly become so popular, we might have stayed where we were.

But we didn't, and maybe we escaped just in time.

We had always lived in or near cities. City kids, as the saying goes. But a few years ago, we cut the cord and headed for the Mendocino coast north of San Francisco. We built a house on a bluff overlooking the ocean.

Soon after it had been completed, we had a party for all our San Francisco friends and a lady from New York who had obviously not been interviewed by Gallup.

She stood with me on our deck, the wind making a mess of her hair, and looked at the waves pounding against the rock cliffs, the grass blowing in the meadow below, the headlands that framed the mouth of the Gualala river, the long beach awash with white sea foam, the blue heron flying by.

"It's beautiful," she said finally, "gorgeous . . . but . . ."

She turned to me. "But gawd, what will you *do*? How will you *survive*?"

She shivered then and hurried back inside where there was a fire burning, martinis were plentiful and the other guests were talking about their days in advertising, the *real* world.

Her concern was not unusual, I have since found out. Her question is one we have often heard, and it is not easy to answer.

Is it possible to escape to a far less complicated way of life and emotionally "survive," as she put it?

For some people, yes. For others? No way.

2

ENISLED BEYOND TIME

I suppose, for us, Robinson Jeffers started it all when he "hung
stones in the sky," built his tower on the Carmel coast and later wrote
a poem to his wife, Una.

> Tonight, dear,
> Let's forget all that, that and the war,
> And enisle ourselves a little beyond time,
> You with this Irish whiskey, I with red wine,
> While the stars go over the sleepless ocean,
> And sometime after midnight I'll pluck you a wreath
> Of chosen ones; we'll talk of love and death,
> Rock-solid themes, old and deep as the sea,

Admit nothing more timely, nothing less real
While the stars go over the timeless ocean,
And when they vanish we'll have spent the night well.

These are the lines I always remember when I think of Jeffers. His monumental poems of stark and terrible tragedy, *Tamar*, *The Women of Point Sur*, *Cawdor*, are long forgotten . . . except the black, brooding essence of them.

To be enisled a little beyond time . . . to watch the stars go over the sleepless ocean . . . ah yes, that was the fascinating idea. A little whiskey? A bit of red wine? Why not?

The idea sat there for many years in the backs of our heads, alive but undemanding. Meanwhile, we moved from Minneapolis to San Francisco, then to New York, then back to San Francisco, then back to New York and, after a final year and a half, cashed in our chips, retired from the advertising business and headed east for San Francisco again . . . that is, we took the long way home by going around the world.

This whole yo-yo operation lasted too many years. By the time we were ready to act, Jeffers' "coast crying out for tragedy" had hollered enough to attract it. Hordes of people had poured into the Carmel area; hundreds of houses had been built; freeways now laced the pine-covered hills. For Jeffers, it would have been a total calamity. For us? Well, I admire Carmel for keeping a lot of its early charm, but, admit it, the struggle is a losing one.

So we began to look north from San Francisco along the Sonoma and Mendocino coasts. Here were cliffs and beaches and rocky coves, pines and meadows and redwoods, sheep ranches and old lumber towns. There weren't many people. Ironically, one kind of exploitation had prevented another. The lumber industry, busily slashing away, had been a deterrent to tourists and overdevelopment. Nobody cared much about sharing the narrow roads with huge, roaring logging trucks.

This was redwood country and still is.

The big, smoke-belching, rusty sawdust burners along Highway 1 were hardly picture postcard attractions. There really weren't many places to stay.

But we liked it and finally bought a lot in the town of Gualala about 125 miles north of the city. It sat in a grove of small and huge Bishop pines at the top of a bluff overlooking a meadow that ran to cliffs that held back the Pacific. Beyond the cliffs the view stretched all the way to Japan.

That night, to celebrate the purchase, we bought a bottle of Irish whiskey and we pushed our way through the trees and the tall grass to the top of the bluff; our bluff now. The stars were there, a whole skyful of them. What's more, a waning moon lit up the sleepless ocean. The surf was gentle, making little slapping noises. We poured our drinks and sat for an hour or so.

It was too nice to talk about anything, even rock-solid themes.

But the dew was heavy and, even with the whiskey, it was soon too wet and chilly to stay until the stars vanished.

We used the lot mostly for picnics for a couple of years . . . wine, sourdough bread, cheese, that sort of thing. We sat behind a screen of small pines in the sun and summer winds, and on foggy days when the gunmetal ocean undulated gently, and on winter days when the clouds towered in the sky and storms scudded by near the horizon or approached head-on with breathtaking violence, and on spring days when the whales played fifty yards offshore.

Studying a lot in all seasons is a procedure I can recommend if you ever decide to buy on the coast. That lovely knoll on the north end of a headland may be utterly dreamy on a warm fall day, but when the summer winds gust up to thirty knots or the winter rain comes sheeting in vertically, the house you build had better be made of heavy stone or your dishes will rattle in the cupboards.

The Pacific does not always live up to its name.

A fellow up the road a piece was fascinated by the way the waves dashed against his cliffs. He constructed a special deck anchored firmly to the rocks so he could sit out there, feel the spray and pretend he

6

was a ship captain, I guess. The deck lasted a couple of years, and he'll show you sadly what's left of it down on the beach, a pile of broken timbers and rusting nails.

"You're certainly going to have floor-to-ceiling windows," our friends used to say when they joined us for picnics. We certainly are not, I decided, after some investigation. Huge expanses of glass may give a dramatic view, but they have to be washed when the salt spray coats them, and the sun can be blinding during the summer, sucking color out of rugs and furniture as if it were soda pop.

Many of our neighbors keep their floor-to-ceiling curtains drawn most of the day.

We settled for two large windows, one angled north, the other south, with a fireplace between. The views are spectacular, framed by redwood walls. The sun rarely beats directly into the house, and we feel well protected when the barometer starts to drop.

One bit of local lore. Areas near the ocean which have trees growing on them usually have better weather than those which don't. Bishop pines are smarter than people, except real estate salesmen.

About the weather in general. It's far better than we expected. We had thought the north coast was fogbound in summer and as wet as Seattle in the winter. It isn't. There is far less fog than there is in San Francisco by a good margin, and when it comes, it's balmy and welcome. The fog bank arcs out into the ocean most of the time and heads down toward the Golden Gate. Those winter news broadcasts we used to hear when San Francisco was clear, "It's raining on the north coast," were perfectly true. The storms hit this area first, but they end here first, too, and we'll often have sunny days when San Francisco and Marin County are being drenched to a fare-thee-well.

The average yearly rainfall along the ocean is 30 inches, a bit more than in San Francisco. Up in the hills it's double that, of course, as is true along the entire Pacific coast. The temperature by the ocean rarely goes above the low seventies or drops below freezing. Go inland a mile and it's much warmer and colder.

There are years, however, when all the averages go out the window. We chose one to build . . . the rainiest winter in history.

"WHAT AM I
DOING HERE?"

I can often remember sitting in interminable advertising meetings, staring dazedly at the wall and wondering, "What am I *doing* here?"

I was to ask myself the same question many times in the next few months, especially when I was balanced on top of an eight-foot stepladder trying to obliterate footprints that had somehow walked across large areas of stained beams.

I suppose the answer in the meeting room was I was trying to earn a living.

The answer on the stepladder was equally simple. I was trying to keep the living I'd earned from disappearing before my eyes.

It wasn't supposed to be that way. We had worked carefully with a local designer we both liked immensely. He was experienced and cooperative and in complete sympathy with building a good, solid house but certainly not a pretentious one.

When the plans were finished, his estimate seemed a bit high but manageable. We put our house in Marin on the market, gritted our teeth, and the plans were sent out for bids.

Our house sold speedily at what seemed to us a fair enough price.

Then the bids on our cottage by the sea came in.

The two highest were more than double the designer's estimate. Even the lowest was sixteen thousand dollars over his calculation. He was as appalled as we were.

Almost, anyway.

Two things had happened. The cost of lumber had suddenly sky-rocketed. Too much redwood had been sent to Japan, or some such thing, and there was a shortage. Also, a "Coastal Protection Initiative" had raised its ugly or beautiful head and appeared to be qualifying for the November ballot. Everyone who had planned to build in the area went into high gear. Contractors had a field day, and the air began to be filled with the echoing crack of hammers.

"All you'll really have to do," the designer had assured us originally, "is go away, come back, and we'll turn the key over to you."

All I did was buy a pair of Levi's and go back to work at a job I knew absolutely nothing about.

I found a contractor in Petaluma about eighty miles away. He was a nice guy who was between houses and wanted to keep his crew working. He liked the coast, figured he'd get in a little fishing, pick up a few abalones and case out the region.

"Why don't I come up and put up the shell," he suggested.

"What's the shell?"

"That's the basic house . . . the foundation, the walls, the roof, the

10

windows, the wiring, the rough plumbing. You finish the rest your-self."

"Hey, I can't pound a nail without bending it."

"Get local people. I'll give you the names of some subcontractors. I'd use them myself if I were doing it. You contract the rest after I finish, maybe do some painting or whatever. Might be fun if you've got the time."

I had the time. I had the Levi's. And I also had a belly full of ap-prehension.

But his price seemed reasonable, and I said okay, let's go.

Our troubles had just begun, his as well as mine. This was roughly the middle of July. The contractor figured he'd have the house up in a couple of months, and we'd be able to move in by Christmas with any luck at all. But he hadn't reckoned with changing times. The sudden rush of activity to beat any possible restrictions the Coastal Initiative might bring had swamped the building permit people. Usually, approval takes a week or so. This time, it took two and a half months . . . the nicest time of the year to build.

The permit finally came in well before the Initiative was voted on, but the great Pacific High that keeps out the storms weakened pre-maturely that year. The first rain came early, and the ground was already wet when the time came to clear the lot.

We knew every tree almost by name and were determined to cut as few as possible, certainly none of the larger ones. This meant we had to position the garage some distance from the house, even though it meant carrying groceries fifty or sixty feet through the wet of winter. One of the trees had a limb that arced gracefully to within a few feet of the ground and then bushed up like a huge pom-pom of long, green needles.

"In no way," my wife said grimly, "is anyone going to touch that limb."

We had to curve the driveway around it, and one of the car stalls is

11

now a bit tricky to back out of. But the limb is there, looking like one you might find in a Japanese print.

The chain saws arrived.

Now then. It is well known that the automobile industry does not build cars for transportation alone. They're also built to express a man's personality.

Psychologists (and copywriters) have had a lot of fun with this.

The fat, balding man driving a *Fury* or a *Mustang* or a *Cougar* is not the man you see but the man *he* sees.

Varoooom.

I really don't think it's as simple as amateur Freudians would have us believe, though maybe it is.

But one machine that's so macho it's almost pornographic is the chain saw.

Wow. Have you ever watched a guy's eyes light up when he gets his saw going, throttles it down to an earsplitting roar and then looks at a tree? That ain't gentle affection shining, brother.

Unlike the Detroit manipulators, the chain saw people haven't been wise enough to use provocative names. McCulloch, Homelite, John Deere are all respected companies, but think how much better their sales might be if they named their models?

"Jack the Ripper" I'm sure would catch many an eye.

Or how about "The Violator" or "The Torrid Tamer"?

We had planned to stay and supervise, trusting no one. But when the saws began to bite and branches began to squeal, crack and crash, we fled to the bar at the Gualala Hotel.

It's only about a quarter mile down wind, and we could still hear the relentless whine of the whirling chains as we downed two martinis which were no more help than ice water.

We stayed away for a week or so, winding up our affairs in Marin, finding a small place to rent on The Sea Ranch, getting settled. When we returned, there was a movable toilet on the back of the lot, a small camper had been parked under the trees where the crew slept and ate,

12

the foundation was in, framing had started . . . and neighbors had begun to complain.

In clearing the lot only the necessary trees had been cut, but the debris had all been pushed to the front, part of it down to the meadow we didn't own. It lay there a sodden, ugly mass of twisted limbs, branches and muddy topsoil. The guy who owned the meadow wasn't at all happy. Our neighbor next door was kind but allowed as how it didn't improve the view from his windows much.

"Why . . . in *hell* . . . did you leave it there?" I asked the foreman.

"Had to get the forms up, the concrete truck was coming," he said, as if any fool would know that.

"Yeah, but how do we get it out? The house is in the way."

"Hmmm. Maybe we could cut down some more trees and drag it around?"

"No way." This from my wife.

"Maybe we could get a truck down there and haul it out?"

"No road," I said.

"It's kind of a problem," the foreman agreed, shaking his head. Then he went back to cutting a two-by-four with his Skil saw.

"Now what, oh hardy pioneer?" my wife said sweetly.

"I'll think about it."

We all did for a couple of months. Then I called a guy who lived back in the hills (a dropout real estate broker, believe it or not) who wanted work.

"No problem," he said, surveying the mess. "All we need is a couple of old truck tires."

"Truck tires?"

"Best way," he said. He had a massive beard, and I *think* he grinned. "We'll put the tires down, build the fire over them and burn the stuff. The tires get hotter'n hell and hold their heat. Keeps everything going. It'll cost you a few bucks, but it shouldn't take too long."

He and a friend came with axes and tires the next morning and had the whole thing cleaned up in a day and a half.

The scar where the fire burned has completely disappeared. Out of

13

the ashes have grown wild irises, Indian paint brush, lupine and rattle-snake grass. In fact, the whole bluff is a natural garden of wildflowers.

Meanwhile, the house went up rapidly enough, and we came to have a great admiration for the crew. It consisted of the foreman, another journeyman carpenter, an apprentice and a helper. The rain, which was coming down almost constantly now, didn't seem to bother them much. They kept plugging away unless a storm got completely out of hand, which it often did.

The big job was to get the roof up and shingled so they could work inside under some cover. The roof was to be supported by three six-inch by ten-inch beams raised at least twenty feet in the air at the peak point. Heavy monsters. I don't know what they weighed, but if I said a quarter of a ton, I couldn't be too far wrong. They had to be stained before they went up, my responsibility.

I hired a local guy who came in with a motor-driven spray, and I began to see what being a contractor meant. You need something done. You look around for someone who says he can do it. You hope he can. You agree on a figure. He goes to work. If the job is done well, you pay him. If it isn't, you argue.

I honestly didn't have to argue much. The few times I did I found I wasn't very good at it.

The painter sprayed everything nicely, including a foot or so of the formed shower that was standing ridiculously in the area that would be the second-floor bathroom. Bathtubs and showers, I found out, go in long before anything else of any importance. If a builder waits until the walls are closed in, he can't get them through the door.

My wife looked at the beams and frowned. "I didn't know they were going to be so dark. They're almost *black*."

"Charcoal, dear. They'll look great against the fir ceiling. You'll see."

"Couldn't you have thinned it out some?"

"I wasn't here when he did it. Come on, I think they look fine."

As I said, I was beginning to understand what being a contractor meant.

We hit a few days of fine weather, and when I came by late one morning, the beams were up . . . big, black triangles in the sky. How those four guys ever did it without a crane I'll never know. They sat there with bulged eyeballs and had nothing to say.

I went to the rear of the lot and piled some lumber scraps I was saving for kindling.

I looked again.

The beams did look pretty black at that.

MIKE AND CATHY

Christmas came and with it a couple of weeks of sunshine . . . but the crew had disappeared.

They were down in Petaluma working on another job.

I couldn't really blame the contractor. I'm sure he had written off the possibility of much profit on his venture in Mendocino. Whenever he came up, usually with a load of lumber, or windows, or pipes, he'd stand in the rain and mutter about the two-month delay in getting the permit.

He was not alone. The bureaucracy had slowed to a pitiful creep. Still we had our permit. Many people weren't to get theirs for a couple of years. Some haven't yet.

17

I found a mason to build the fireplace. He came to work each day with his two young kids who managed to track concrete over the entire house.

But it was fun to watch the big stones being fitted. Since they were all shapes and sizes, it took a great deal of skill. The guy had it, and a good eye as well.

The house we were living in had a fireplace, too, one of those hanging iron things in the center of the room with a hood and long stack topped by a screening device that turned in the wind. It turned all right with a maddening squeak, and only about half the smoke went up the stack.

It was our only source of heat except for a few small electric units scattered around that sometimes worked and sometimes didn't. The house was cute, but cozy it wasn't . . . not on nights when the temperature dropped to freezing.

As I have noted, the farther away from the ocean you get the colder it is.

My first job in the morning was to get the fire going, turn on all the burners on the kitchen stove and plug in the coffee pot.

The plank flooring, which we had planned to have in our house, was cold as a headstone in a cemetery. We decided to switch to carpeting, and, as commercials sometimes say, we're glad we did.

When the mason finished his work and stood back admiring it with good reason, I was not to be overwhelmed by the beauty of it all.

"Before you leave," I said, "we're testing it."

"Sure, of course." He looked a bit hurt.

I opened the damper, rolled some balls of paper and tossed them onto the virgin yellow fire bricks. When I lit them, they burned briskly. Not a puff of smoke came out into the room.

"See?" he said happily.

"We're not finished yet," I muttered.

I found some scraps of lumber, built a small fire. It soon was blazing merrily. No smoke.

"See?" he said again.

"We're not finished yet." By now I knew all about wet wood. I got a couple of small logs that had been soaking in the rain and tossed them on. This time there was plenty of smoke. It all went up the chimney.

"Beautiful," I said and wrote out his final check.

Sooner or later, you'll meet everybody in Gualala at the post office along about 11:30 when the mail is distributed. It's a busy place for an hour or so.

I saw our designer there one day. He'd been keeping an eye on the construction to see that the walls were straight and the lumber was the proper quality.

"Hey," he said. "I've been looking for you. I've got a guy who can help you finish the house."

"How?"

"He can do just about anything. Paneling, trimming, painting, plumbing, papering . . . whatever's needed."

"Carpenter?"

"No, he's an architect. Helps me with plans sometimes. He worked on some of yours as a matter of fact."

My experience with the dropout real estate broker had been fine. Why not?

"When can I see him?"

"I'll send him over this afternoon if you're going to be around."

Mike arrived in an ancient Chevrolet pickup truck, the kind with a round hood that looks almost like a face. From one of the grids protruded a large oval piece of plywood painted red. It hung there like a panting tongue.

He was a tall young guy with a mop of brown curly hair that haloed his head four inches in every direction. No beard. Granny glasses. Blue eyes that watched you carefully and with amusement.

He told me what he could do. There wasn't anything he couldn't.

I must admit I was dubious at first. So many skills, and he couldn't have even been out of school very long. It turned out he was twenty-seven, had decided he didn't care much about drawing plans for super-

19

markets in the Bay Area. He liked to work with his hands. Above all, he loved wood. He lived on a ranch a couple miles up the ridge as sort of caretaker.

"Ranch-sitter," he said.

I liked him. "Okay, let's go."

It was one of the best decisions I've ever made.

By this time redwood paneling had all but disappeared from the market, but I got the last batch the lumber yard had, and it was lovely stuff, clear as a bell, no sap wood, packaged in huge cartons. We piled it all in the center of the living room. None of it was going to get water stained if we could help it.

The contractor's crew came back. The walls were insulated, the plasterboard put up, the bedrooms finished. They were working fast now. We could sense that time had run out for them.

Most of the days the rain beat down steadily. Arc lamps lit the rooms. A large oil heater blasted away. The back lot was full of deep ruts filled with water. The camper had begun to list to starboard. The sea was stained brown from the rushing flood of the Gualala River and jammed with logs, trees and branches that bobbed around dismally and crashed against the cliffs.

A lot of driftwood was born that winter.

I know it was no longer fun for the crew. They were grim-faced, short-tempered. One night, something had to give. I don't know all the details, but I will speculate that they went to the bar at the Gualala Hotel, a friendly place, well-stocked. At some point, along toward midnight, they had a great idea. They'd drive up the small road that skirts the river and see what was going on.

There's nothing up there much but second-growth redwood and a campground, pretty enough in summer but no place to be at that time. All went well for a mile or so. Then they drove down a hill and into water and mud as high as the truck's hubcaps. The truck wouldn't budge. They decided to stick it out. Why get wet? Maybe the water would go down.

Instead it rose steadily, and they finally had to wade ashore awash to their armpits.

It took most of the next day to get the truck hauled out and dry enough to start.

It was now mid-February. They soon finished their work and took off down Highway 1. Did they pause to watch the sun sink into the blue Pacific? I doubt it very much.

I did, though. I stood there in the dim light of the unfinished house and looked out the window. Whatever happened now was my responsibility.

I turned around and looked up at the beams.

They sure were black.

The cross beam at the apex of the roof reminded me of something. Oh yes, a scaffold . . . one that would turn on any hangman in the world.

When we arrived late in the morning the next day, the air was filled with symphony music coming from a small FM radio. Mike was half way up a ladder nailing a piece of paneling to the wall. With him was a girl with long blond hair, a lovely face. She was wearing a faded pink sweat shirt, torn jeans and rubber boots.

"This is Cathy," Mike said, "my helper."

A good share of one wall had already been finished, and it looked fine. Mike glued each redwood strip in place first, then nailed it, then countersank the nails . . . a rarity in care these slam-bang days. Cathy handed him the pieces, even cut some to fit.

They seemed to know exactly what they were doing . . . and why.

My wife started staining the doors. Solid ash they were, one extravagance we hadn't cut. She used the same stain that had gone on the beams, but *thinned out*, she emphasized pointedly. The result was great. The grain pattern emerged clearly, and the color went beautifully with the redwood. I started to paint one of the bedrooms, beginning to feel a flow of enthusiasm for the first time in weeks.

21

The fog arrives on big cat feet.

We grew our house among the pines.

Succulents grow to giant size.

23

Mike and Cathy's cottage in the woods.

Wood burning stoves are practical as well as attractive.

Photo by Julie Verran

The truck named "Licky-Lips."

Photo by Julie Verran

Cathy and Mike.

Mike did love wood, and he continued to work carefully. All the trim fit, the window sills were rounded off at the corners, the banister up the stairs was rounded off, too, sanded smooth and later oiled. Screws were countersunk and the holes filled with wooden plugs. He also built two window seats, bookcases, a fireplace mantel, cases for the phonograph speakers and a railing for the balcony more attractive than any we've ever seen.

If you ever contract your own house and are lucky enough to find a Mike, you won't have too much trouble.

Actually, the rest of the work is really not too difficult. The plumber comes with the sinks, water heater and other appliances and puts them in. He doesn't need any help. The electrician's done it all before, too. He wires the light fixtures you've picked out. The lamp store will give you good advice, and you'll get a reasonable discount if you buy everything at one place. The mirror man brings the mirrors, puts them up. And finally, happiest of days, the rug man comes, the carpeting and vinyl go down amazingly swiftly, and suddenly you're at home.

Meanwhile, of course, you've signed enough checks to fill a paper sack.

Our days with Mike and Cathy were pleasant and productive. We had some laughs, a few serious discussions, enjoyed picnics on the deck in the sun. (Yes, it did begin to shine.) But most of the joy came in watching someone work as if what he did was important to him.

Mike has since built a shop where he builds furniture and powers his equipment with a gasoline-driven generator. Cathy has designed some hand puppets that are so attractive they have been picked up by a manufacturer on a royalty basis.

We still see the old Chevrolet pickup truck around. The original tongue has been replaced by a bright new one.

We moved in on April 15 and had our first visitors a week later. A girl from Sweden who had lived with us for about a year as an exchange student arrived with her husband. She looked around inside and said with just a hint of a Scandinavian lilt, "Oh, Roger . . . it's beautiful. It looks just like a sculpture."

She couldn't have said anything nicer.

Okay. I'll get to the bottom line. Was all the work worth it? Did we meet our original estimate?

To answer the second question first, no we didn't. But I know we saved at least ten thousand dollars on the lowest bid and probably a lot more. Who knows what additional costs there would have been if we had accepted. No one I've ever known has escaped without them.

Was it worth it?

Well, the black beams don't remind me of a gallows any longer. I kinda feel they're part of me.

WATCHERS ON
THE BLUFF

One of the amusing reactions to living here is surprise that the ocean doesn't go away.

Each morning we look, and there it is again.

It still astonishes us.

I suppose this is so because most of our visits to various seasides in the past were relatively brief. When our holiday was over, we'd return to some city or other, and the ocean became a memory, recalled, even longed for, from time to time, but really part of another world.

Here it *is* the world, dominant, inescapable.

Our view of it is one of about 180 degrees. To the southeast is a mile-long beach ending at the Gualala Point headland. Straight ahead are the rocks of Robinson's Reef. To the northwest is another headland and beyond it the light tan cliffs of Fish Rock where the seals live. The horizon, twelve miles out, has a definite curve.

The view is so immense it almost ceases to be a view. It becomes a total environment. One does feel *drawn in*, at times no longer a watcher on the bluff but another creature of the sea.

"In a few more years we'll be growing kelp for hair," I sometimes say.

I laugh, of course.

But not too loudly.

Enough of this. Watchers on the bluff we are, and what we see is fascinating.

In the spring and early summer, cormorants nest in the cliffs high enough to be out of reach of the waves and usually under some protruding ledge that affords protection from egg-stealing predators. I've seen ravens hang almost motionless in the air above the nests, but I have yet to see a successful egg-snatch. There must be some, though.

Ever so often one of the cormorant pair flies frantically out over the ocean, wings beating furiously, long neck protruding. You would think it was heading for China, but, a few hundred feet out, it circles sharply and comes flying back just as frantically to land again by the nest.

The performance is probably some age-old proclamation of territory.

Or maybe the bird just wants to relieve the boredom.

Or maybe it just wants to relieve *itself*, for such an occurrence always seems to accompany the ritual.

Other seasons of the year cormorants spend a lot of time sitting in groups on rocks, their heads turning from side to side. They are definitely sea birds. I've never seen one flying over land, although they may do so for all I know.

In June the brown pelicans return, gliding by in long sinuous lines. They seem as sedate and composed as the cormorants are nervous. They pass us by for several days until one group of six that seems to have chosen this spot for its own each year arrives and settles in. They fish by circling twenty or thirty feet above the water, pausing suddenly, then sideslipping with a crash into the waves. Gulls, no fools, hang around and snatch at pieces of the catch, sometimes even stealing from a pelican's beak.

The big birds pay little attention to their tormentors.

We share the bluff and meadow with a pair of ravens we have named "Never" and "More." They often circle in front of our windows, feathers ruffled by the wind, legs hanging down with claws extended, looking as evil as their age-old reputation.

From primitive times, man has invested ravens with sinister powers. They were semi-sacred to the Greeks, the early Norsemen, the Zuni of New Mexico and were always feared as creatures from the nether regions.

They certainly should be feared by other birds who live nearby, if not the cormorants. We often see them with eggs or young birds stolen from nests. The anguished parents who give noisy chase never seem able to harm them. More dedicated watchers than I say ravens are always able to avoid the claws and beaks of their attackers, swerving the last moment or simply moving their heads like a good boxer avoiding a blow.

They also eat offal and shellfish cast up on shore as well as insects, and they have been known to carry off young chickens.

Still, we're sorta fond of them.

They're quite beautiful if you care to look. They have lustrous black feathers with a steel-blue and purplish irridescence. Their throat feathers are light gray, bills and feet black, and they fly with skill rivaling a gull's.

They're known to be one of the most highly developed birds there are . . . quick-witted, cunning, audacious.

31

Ravens are believed to live as long as a hundred years and remain mated for life, renewing their vows every spring with a kind of silly airborne dance, turning somersaults, trying to fly on their backs and making gurgling noises.

For more than a year now, I've been trying to photograph one of them close up in flight. I can't tell which is which. Males and females look much alike. But they're both too smart for me.

They'll be flying just outside. The moment I open the door, they sail off in the wind. I've tried hiding under the deck. They're not fooled a bit. I've tried crouching in a pine grove, camera ready. All I ever got was a sore back.

Off in the distance I can always hear them "krawk, quawk, quawk" derisively.

I'm sure they know they'll be here, unphotographed, long after I'm dead.

Almost every morning in the fall, about second cup of coffee time, we are visited by band-tailed pigeons. Fifteen or twenty fly out of the woods, circle over the house, race hell-bent for the ocean, turn sharply, proceed for a hundred yards along the edge of the cliffs, then arc high in the golden air and disappear back over the trees.

In a few minutes they return, but this time thirty strong, and, as they circle, they are joined by other band-tails until on a good day there may be as many as a hundred.

It's quite a sight. The birds are mostly gray with white crescents at the backs of their necks and dark bands across their tails. They don't glide like gulls or ravens. Their wing beat is swift and steady, and they swerve with a darting speed that would put O. J. Simpson to shame. No wonder hunters have a hard time hitting them.

Usually, the flock circles for ten or fifteen minutes, then disperses and soon is gone. But on certain days something puzzling happens. One bird will plummet to the ground and land with a great flutter and spread of tail precisely at the edge of the cliff. It will soon be joined by others, finally the whole flock.

Combers charge in like cavalry, plumed and fierce.

There the birds sit in a long row, like kids in a theater gallery, and look out at the ocean.

Why? It seems to have nothing to do with food. They can't be watching for surf fish. Their diet is seeds and berries, plentiful back in the hills.

They simply seem to enjoy the view.

Their fascination isn't quickly satisfied. They will stay at the top of the cliff, or just below it, as long as half an hour, fluttering a bit to change position, sometimes moving twenty yards or so, but generally remaining reasonably quiet.

Why? again.

But, on second thought, why puzzle about it?

What difference does it make? The band-tails watch the sea; we watch the band-tails, and all of us have a fine time.

The osprey is considered an endangered species, but there are quite a few who live on the Mendocino coast. A pair nests near us.

When daddy goes a-hunting in the morning, it's like watching fate.

The bird flies powerfully with huge sweeping wing beats out over the ocean. It stays fairly high, from fifty to a hundred feet, and covers a wide area looking for fish near the surface. It seems to have great patience and is ready to wait until just the right situation occurs, for, unlike sea birds, its feathers have no protecting oil. It can't float or swim. An accident would mean bye, bye, osprey.

Often the hawk will circle half an hour, flying several miles, before it suddenly pauses, hovers, then plunges into the water feet first. There is a big splash. The bird often goes completely under.

When it surfaces, a struggle begins. Its wings that spread as much as six feet beat the water and air, and, for an agonizing moment, it seems as if it will never fight its way aloft. But it does, and clutched in its talons is usually a fish, sometimes as long as the bird's body. The fish, I must emphasize, is far from dead. It thrashes and wiggles like a trout on a hook. Bit by bit the osprey gains altitude, but it's up hill all the way.

When the hunter lumbers overhead on the way to its nest, its prey is fairly quiet . . . or shocked out of its wits.

I sometimes wince in sympathy.

Imagine suddenly being plucked out of your own universe and finding yourself suspended in an alien sky you never knew existed!

During daylight hours, there's never a time that there isn't a pattern of gulls somewhere in view.

What marvelous fliers they are! They circle high in the bright air, or bob along the cliffs catching updrafts or glide, even into a stiff wind, hardly moving their wings at all.

I'm convinced that a good share of the time they fly just for the sheer joy of it.

I've seen a group of them almost dance their way up the coast into a breeze, then climb a hundred feet, peel off one at a time and sail back with the wind at their tails. It was almost like watching skiers go up a hill and then take off down the slope.

Anchor Bay beach at sunset.

Even in winter when the rain is pounding down, they're out there big as life.

In the spring and late fall come the great migrations. The sky is alive with gulls, usually flying fairly close to or above the shoreline. Farther out are ducks, huge V's of geese, silvery patches of sandpipers. The whole bird world seems on the move.

Once, early in October, a storm drove the migrants in from the ocean. There were thousands. I estimated that more than three hundred gulls passed our window in about one minute, some as close as twenty feet away. Among them were flocks of Bonaparte's gulls, much smaller than the Western, California and glaucous-winged gulls we usually see. They look more like terns, and they seem to have no fear at all of landing on stormy seas. The waves were coming in twenty feet high, but the little birds rode the combers until the crests broke over their heads.

There was just too much good food coming down from the flooding river.

People who live near Fish Rock at Anchor Bay are often kept awake by the barking of seals. Quite a large colony lives there during the summer, and some of them visit us from time to time . . . groups of two or three or loners. They play in the surf, ride the waves and stick their sleek heads out of the water to see what's going on.

If you stand at the top of the cliffs, you can often find one floating close to the rocks below and staring up at you with large liquid eyes. Its expression is one of benign friendliness and perhaps amusement at seeing such a peculiar animal as you.

Such pleasant meetings always remind me of a bit in Victor B. Scheffer's splendid book, *The Year of the Seal,* published by Charles Scribner's Sons:

> In the mythos of the folk who make their living from the sea it is well known that hidden in the dark pools of the eyes of certain seals are spirits that call out to certain men. The Irish among us, and a few Scandinavians who have lived long at the edge of the sea, can hear the message best. These seals, they say, are really fisherfolk who were caught in some act of displeasing the gods and were made to live in hairy skins forever after and to wander at the will of the winds and the tides. Once in a while such a seal will save the life of a drowning sailor and will then be released from its beastly bindings. It will turn into a beautiful maid and will become the sailor's wife, but there will be no offspring from the union, and the old women in the village will know the reason why. Always dark-brown of eye and soft of body these beautiful creatures are, and they lie awake in bed when the full moon streams through the window.
>
> And their feet are a bit colder than the feet of ordinary women.

Lovely they may be, but they sometimes display a ferocity that is chilling to watch. Seals usually feed under water except when they attack a fish that is too large to gulp. Then they bring it to the surface. Once we saw one with a lingcod that must have been a yard long. The seal had a tight grip around its belly, and it shook the fish like a bull terrier, biting a large chunk out of it. Then it dived, came up under the fish and tossed it into the air. Again, a piece of the fish disappeared.

By this time the ever-alert gulls had gathered around and were squawking and feasting on the bloody debris. Again and again the fish was attacked until it no longer existed.

The seal swam off, the gulls flew away and the indifferent ocean flowed undisturbed. It all took only a few minutes.

Certainly the most fantastic show we see is the parade of the gray whales.

In November and December they head south, backs rolling, spray spouting, on their way to lagoons on the west coast of Baja California to mate and give birth. They almost always travel about a quarter mile offshore, and binoculars are good to have. They start returning in January in much the same way . . . until the month of May.

Then the females come back with their calves, and they often pause at the mouth of the Gualala River to rest and play in the surf, as close as fifty yards from the beach.

Mothers will stand on their tails thrusting their great heads out of the water for long moments. The calves will leap. You can hear the spray as well as see it. Local whale watchers say the animals like to roll on the sandy bottom to knock the barnacles off. Some say they are attracted by fresh water.

Adult gray whales can weigh up to thirty tons and reach a length of thirty-five to forty-five feet. The youngsters are about a third that size.

They'll often hang around fifteen or twenty minutes. Then the mother seems to say, "Let's get the show on the road," and off they go, heading north again.

Gray whales playing offshore.

On good days the visitations will be repeated a number of times, and, if we have guests, I watch the waters south for a telltale spout. When I see one, I tell my friends I'm going to call a whale in for them.

My incantation is often rewarded, and I'm sure I have convinced many, children especially, that I have magical powers.

I sometimes believe I do myself.

The meadow and bluff are lovely to watch, too . . . if you don't become too involved.

From the moment in late winter when the first wild irises start blooming until the summer sun and winds bring growth pretty much to a stop, a lot goes on, and although it may all seem much the way it has always been, it isn't.

That spot where the Indian paintbrush grew last year can this year be covered by lupine, the orange-red flowers giving way to the blue. And somewhere downwind, where there was only grass before, are clumps of Indian paintbrush.

Dozens of different plants and grasses grow there in a kind of shifting harmony, but a struggle for survival goes on just as decisive as the one beneath the sea.

A couple of summers ago, we noticed a few small plants of California lilac (Ceanothus) on the hill just below us. Their dark green leaves and bright blue blossoms are easily recognized even by amateurs. This spring, they have spread over an area twenty feet square and are heading happily for an empty space where we had to clear some dead trees.

To tell the truth, we cannot even remember what grew in their place before.

Our initial determination to cut as few trees as possible turned out to be something of a mistake. Bull pines grow with astonishing speed, and when they're too crowded, begin to die branch by branch. Several we saved when our lot was cleared have had to be taken down. There are others that should be thinned out for the good of those that remain.

Our early sensitivity has diminished considerably, and we have come to realize that our neighbors who smiled at our don't-touch-a-living-limb attitude were probably right.

My wife's capitulation came even sooner than mine. She arrived one day with a large box so heavy she could hardly carry it.

"A present," she said with a grin, "for you."

It was a small chain saw.

THE SOCIAL RAMBLE

These days, when it's "in" to be "into," the Mendocino coast, if not a hotbed of activity, definitely has warm sheets.

We're into most anything you can name . . . pottery, poetry, photography, painting, weaving, knitting, quilting, macrame, sculpture, music. The woods and bluffs are full of arts and crafts doers.

And they *do* do. Many are exceptionally good.

In our area, all this talent comes into focus largely through the efforts of an organization called Gualala Arts. It now has nearly four hundred members, holds monthly programs, runs a shop in Gualala, The Dolphin, where artists can sell their works, gives scholarships and puts on a yearly show called "Art-in-the-Redwoods" that attracts exhibitors and visitors from all over the state.

On program nights, we all bring our plates and cutlery to the Community Center, a frame building enclosing a small hall with a stage and a kitchen and equipped with folding chairs and tables donated by local citizens over the years. Each chair has a name painted on it to honor its donor.

Usually, too, each family brings a casserole or a salad or a dessert . . . "enough for three times the number in your group."

Potlucks were a new experience for us, and I will admit we were somewhat apprehensive at first, especially my wife. Her concern was not that we wouldn't get a good dinner, but that what she brought wouldn't be good enough.

There was much furrowed-brow searching through cookbooks as each program approached, and I'm sure the same thing was happening in other households, for the food is always imaginative and well prepared.

We discovered that you should approach a potluck with a sense of adventure. The idea is not to look for something you think you might like but try a spoonful of everything you can load on your plate — much as you would at a smorgasbord — and then go back for more. Some of the old hands bring platters instead of plates.

The wine selection is always good. You select your own bottle at home and bring it with you.

Anyone on a diet who exercises some restraint during the early part of the dinner inevitably succumbs when the homemade cakes, pies and cookies appear. Again, you don't settle for one but try several.

I am sometimes amused to look around the room and remember that a good many of those present were once executive types, holding titles and important positions in business, engineering, education, science and even banking. I doubt that any of them, at the height of their careers, could have been driven to a potluck with a bull prod. Yet here they all were sharing the joys of one, not the least of which is a third piece of chocolate fudge cake.

The programs cover a wide range of subjects, most anything relating to the arts or nature. Recently, a Japanese girl who had studied flower arranging in Kyoto for six years and achieved a level of excellence equivalent to a black belt in Judo gave a demonstration. A number of the members brought flowers from their gardens, and some were disappointed that she used so few in each of her arrangements. But striking they were. She also showed us how to put on a kimono which seemed to be fastened with more knots than you'll find in a scout manual.

Another time, there was a showing of vintage W. C. Fields, Buster Keaton and Laurel and Hardy movie shorts. We laughed as hard as we did when we first saw them. Youngsters, anyone under thirty, laughed even harder.

A fellow who makes, restores and repairs spinning wheels explained how they worked. Weavers wove and demonstrated techniques of using vegetable matter for making dyes. A local artist who works in the now rare art of fresco painting explained how she did it. There have been poetry readings. Once we had a dance group. One of the girls was more than slightly pregnant, but she hung in there and was loudly applauded.

At one of the first programs we saw, the star was an amateur photographer whose slide show was billed, "America the Beautiful." His wife, at the piano behind the curtain, opened the program by playing the appropriate song. The first slide was a fine picture of the Statue of Liberty followed by a number of slides of moss-hung trees and azaleas taken at a park near the nation's capital.

Then came a great leap Westward. We were now in the Rockies, and the pictures of mountains and glaciers were breathtaking. Most of the remaining slides were shot in Washington, Oregon and California, states which certainly live up to the show's title. Nobody seemed to mind that a considerable amount of beautiful America had been left out.

The photographer's great interest was taking extreme close-ups of flowers, especially those with dew drops on them. These were remarkable shots, all sharply focused and highly dramatic. He's one of the best dew drop men I've ever seen.

The last slide was a picture of the photographer's granddaughter playing with her cat, and the program ended with the piano again play-ing "America the Beautiful."

We went out into the foggy night feeling good about everything. We hadn't seen one of those horrors Hollywood now calls movies or a television crime show in months, and we didn't miss them a bit.

"We might," I suggested, "stop at the Gualala Hotel." It was really more of a question than anything.

The answer came quickly. "Oh, not tonight. It's Saturday. It'll be jammed. Some other time, huh?"

"Why don't you drop me off? I can get home all right."

"Not without me you don't." This firmly.

Well, it was worth a try.

We walked to the car.

"Incidentally," I said as I unlocked the door, "doesn't a PG rating on a movie really stand for Perfectly Godawful?"

"What has that got to do with it?"

"I don't know," I admitted. "It just occurred to me."

The next month, my wife said, "The Gualala Arts thing is this Saturday. Want to go?"

"Sure, what's on the program?"

"The Madrigals and the Bell Ringers."

"Hey, they're not bringing in rock groups, too!"

"Don't be silly. The Madrigals are six young ladies who specialize in singing seventeenth century pieces. The Bell Ringers are just what they say they are. They ring English hand bells made at the Whitechapel foundry. That's where Big Ben and the Liberty Bell were cast."

"Never heard of 'em."

"Of course you have. I told you all about the Bell Ringers a couple of months ago."

"No, I mean Big Ben and the Liberty Bell."

The Madrigals were fine, poised and confident even though they were somewhat at a disadvantage. Their alto had gone to Kansas City. But the leader, usually a soprano, took her part and did beautifully.

44

The Bell Ringers, including a couple of the Madrigals who doubled in bells, were nine people varying in age from fifteen to sixty. They played music by Schumann, J. S. Bach and Chopin which they had arranged themselves. The little fifteen-year-old, long blond hair, blue jeans and a bright red and white blouse, rang out her parts with authority, right on beat. Her mother, sitting beside us, practically exploded with pride.

Afterwards, everyone was invited to come on stage and try the bells. Quite a few did, donning brown gardening gloves to keep from tarnishing the metal.

I bonged one of the big bongers myself. Very satisfying. The sound, as promised, lasted for almost a minute.

"I suppose," my wife said as we drove out of the parking lot, "you want to go to the Gualala Hotel."

"Now there's an idea! How did you ever think of it?"

"Okay, I'll drop you off. Have fun, but remember you're a watcher on the bluff."

"I'm a bluffer on the watch," I corrected her.

She considered this a moment or two.

"That's the same thing, isn't it?"

"Not quite, but don't worry about it. I'll see you in a couple of hours."

She drove off with a puzzled frown.

Nobody ever wants to watch the action at the Gualala Hotel from any bluff. It's impossible anyway. Once you're in, you're part of it.

Georgia Hesse, travel editor of the *San Francisco Examiner*, who has been around more than any one person has a right to, was once asked to name the ten places she'd most like to revisit. Her list included staying at The Sea Ranch Lodge and spending Saturday night at the Gualala Hotel bar.

It's hard to say what makes it so much fun. The room itself is large and L-shaped and dominated by a long, old-fashioned bar. It has a

Gualala's skyline dominated by its old hotel.

beat-up metal fireplace used for heat and not for atmosphere. On its walls are photographs of people holding steelhead aloft. Chief Justice Earl Warren and the actor, Fred MacMurray, are two easily recognized. There's a juke box, a couple of tables and a few chairs off in corners.

That's it.

It's just a barny old barroom with no pretentions whatsoever.

The juke box was blasting out something about "Leroy Brown, the meanest man in town" when I entered and began to push my way to the bar. The open end of the L was whirling with dancers. Their torsos gyrated in the vague direction of partners, but it was impossible to tell for sure who was dancing with whom. Nor did it seem to matter. The group had a nervous system of its own.

Somebody started stomping. Soon everyone was stomping, and the floor shook.

I finally edged my way in and ordered a drink. The owner and two other bartenders were working at a steady clip. Bottles hardly had a chance to settle into their serving wells before they were lifted again.

The cars parked outside included as many Mercedes and Cadillacs

46

Photo by Nick Carter

as pickup trucks. Inside, it would have been difficult to tell who owned which. A few of the ladies wore pantsuits, most wore jeans or jeans ripped off to make shorts; some wore muumuus and no bras; some even wore dresses . . . and no bras. For the most part, the gals wore their hair cut short, but here and there a bouffant beehive swayed in the smoky air, surprisingly stable under the circumstances.

The chief adornments of the men were mustaches, thick and bushy, of course. They wore everything from T-shirts to open-throated jackets with shell beads. One guy sported a leather vest that revealed hairy arms and considerable belly, equally hairy. He didn't have a partner but danced anyway, his eyes closed, sweat rolling down his cheeks, a half empty beer bottle in his hand.

Was it a young crowd? Yes. Was it an old crowd? Yes, again. Was it a middle-aged crowd? Another yes. It was a kind of everybody happening.

Once in a great while a waltz was played. The dancers bumped their way around one-two-three, looking silly but loving it. When a polka was played, the bottles rattled in the back bar.

Of course, it all had a sexual overtone, but the atmosphere wasn't thick with it. Girls danced with anyone who asked, leaving their purses on the bar. The rest of us swayed back and forth holding our drinks and grinning. Laughter was the loudest sound except for the juke box.

I would imagine that eventually there's a certain amount of pairing up, but that doesn't seem to be the main idea.

Once in a great while there's a beef. Some guy decides to take on some other guy. But these are usually shoving matches and are quickly quieted. Nobody really wants the fun disturbed.

When I woke up the next morning, I could still hear the music of "Leroy Brown" in my head and something else . . . the bong of the big brass bell I'd rung at the Gualala Arts program.

THE UNCOMPLEATED
ANGLER

All summer long the mouth of the Gualala River is closed by a sand-bar, but when the first rains come, and the water begins to rise, it doesn't take long for it to open.

It gets help.

The young and old-time fishermen of the town go down and begin to shovel. The technique is a simple one. Cut a narrow trench through the sand just before a rising evening tide. It need be only a foot or so wide as long as the water starts running. By morning, the action of the ocean and the pressure of the water in the river will have done the job.

The Gualala will be flowing to the sea again through a channel twenty feet or more wide, and there will already be silver salmon and steelhead in the river.

At least that's what happens if all goes well.

Sometimes the process has to be repeated several times. Sometimes the fish just don't come in. But the watch on the Gualala is constant, and news travels fast to the store, the post office and especially to the Gualala Hotel bar.

"Any action?" I asked one of the beer-drinking regulars.

"Naw. The Johnson boy said he lost one this morning. But that's what they all say. Snag a hook and it's always a fish."

"Was he fishing already? Didn't think the steelhead season opened until next Saturday."

"It's okay to take silvers."

"They look pretty much alike, don't they? Silvers and steelhead?"

Slow smile, swallow of beer. "Yeah. No *way* to tell 'em apart . . . before the season opens anyway. You catch a fish down there now, it's a silver. Has to be. You just take him home and eat him." Big laugh.

"Okay, I get it. But seriously, how *do* you tell them apart?"

"Well, what you do is this. You grab the fish by the tail, and if it slips through your hand, it's a steelhead. If it doesn't, it's a silver. Nothing to it."

"You've got to be kidding."

"God's truth. There's a kind of ridge, a flare, on the tail of a salmon. Keeps it from slipping."

One of the other old-timers joined in. "The other way to tell is to look at their mouths. If it's all white, it's a steelhead. If it has some black patches, it's a silver." Pause. "Or is it the other way around?" Another big laugh.

I leave the bar and walk across the road to the top of the bluff over the river. Down below on the rocks a half-dozen teenagers are casting spinners out into the smooth water. Four or five Labradors are running around being excited and silly. The sun hangs low in the sky, and the light is yellow-gold.

50

I stand beside an old man who's been keeping an eye on things.

"Seen any?"

"Couple."

"Hey," I said, "there's one over there." Across the river had been a flash; the water roiled, and now ripples were running toward the shore and out into the river.

"Silver," the old man said. "Nice one."

"Silver," I agreed without a moment's hesitation. "No doubt about it."

When the salmon boats circle a mile offshore during most of the summer, I'm glad I'm not on one. I know I'd be staring glassy-eyed at the horizon trying to keep my stomach from turning over, and the struggle has never been worth it. I always lose.

Oh, I've caught salmon a few times . . . once a forty pounder. But sitting on a party boat dragging a three-pound weight for half a day transported into a new dimension of misery is not my idea of either sport or fun.

Watching the kids fishing was intriguing, however.

This was something you could do with your feet on the ground. It reminded me of casting for bass from the banks of a glass-smooth lake I once lived on in Minnesota. There, I could arrive home after work, flip a plug out along the lily pads and catch a fish every three or four tries. The bass exploded out of the water like big-mouthed politicians. In twenty minutes, I'd have enough for dinner. After cleaning the fish, there was always plenty of time to catch the silver martini, a species on which there was no limit at all. It was hardly endangered.

I drove to Point Arena and bought a license. I bought a pole, a reel, fifty yards of line, some leaders, a knife and three spinners guaranteed to be killers by my friends at the bar.

Despite all the expert information I'd received, I still wasn't sure I could really tell the difference between a silver and a steelhead, so I waited until the season officially opened. When I clomped down to the river late in the afternoon, the sky was overcast, and I was not alone.

51

There were half a dozen campers parked on the flats, cars and pick-up trucks dotted the scene. At least fifty fishermen—man, boy and lady—were standing on the sand beach and whipping the water with their lines. Some, of course, were dressed in waders and stood in the stream up to their bellies.

I joined the crowd, found a place and had at it. My first few casts were a bit embarrassing, but I soon caught the swing of it and sent my blue spinner arcing to the deep part of the river. I wound it in fairly rapidly. That seemed to be the prevailing technique. Get it out there, get it back, get it out there, get it back.

I suppose a steelhead swimming upstream eventually gets annoyed enough to strike at anything.

None did anywhere that I could see.

I caught a nice long string of weeds, cleaned it off. My hands were wet and cold. I dried them on my handkerchief, wishing I'd brought a towel.

I stood there, hands in pockets, and watched for a while. The rods flashed in the air, the reels spun, the spinners plopped into the water running darkly. Each fisherman seemed alone in his cocoon of concentration. Down the stream there was a flash and a splash.

"Son of a bitch," someone said. "Did you see the son of a bitch? Son of a bitch!"

One, at least, was coming.

Fifty lines sailed across the water, including mine. I was pleased with my cast. The spinner almost reached the opposite shore. I wound in slowly, then swiftly, then slowly, giving the lure some of my old Minnesota know-how. Nothing happened, except that a drizzle began to fall.

I brought the rod back slowly and sent the spinner high and far. Long before it reached its appointed spot it dropped to the water. My line had backlashed, but good. I tugged at the tangle, tried to unwind the line. It was stuck, and would move only a foot or two in either direction.

Patience. I know that a backlash, if fiddled with enough, will suddenly loosen, and all will be well again. This one didn't. My glasses began to mist over. My hands were now numb. Rain was dripping down the back of my neck. Finally, I took out my knife and cut the line. No amount of yanking would budge the spinner. It was firmly caught in the rocks at the bottom of the river where I'm sure it is to this day.

By the time I reached my car, my boots were thick with gray mud. I cleaned them off as best I could with bunches of wet grass and headed home. I hoped my wife would have built a nice fire, but she hadn't.

One thing I know. The steelhead that splashed downstream wasn't caught . . . at least then. It had time enough to get up river before I left.

But not too much, at that.

The rain continued, and the river was too muddy for fishing for a couple of weeks. Then one thing led to another. And . . . well, I didn't try again.

But I haven't given up. They do catch steelhead in the Gualala, and beautiful they are . . . eighteen or twenty pounders. I've seen several and heard, of course, about several hundred. But I'm a believer, and there's another season coming.

I talked with an old golf-playing buddy of mine in San Francisco. He *says* he's an expert steelhead fisherman and that I was doing it all wrong.

"Spinners are for the birds. You need salmon eggs, *fresh* salmon eggs. You let 'em roll down the bottom of the stream as naturally as possible. Steelhead can't resist 'em. Once you've caught one, you'll never be the same. It's the greatest sport there is."

He also advised me to get waders, a special fly rod, tapered lines, a new reel . . . the works. "Two or three hundred bucks ought to cover it," he said.

I've been thinking about it.

I'm not sure where I'd get fresh salmon eggs that time of year. I've looked in the stores, and they carry small jars of something that *looks* like salmon roe. But the labels don't claim it is.

Fishing on the Gualala river.

I did see something that fascinates me. It's a lure called the "Arkansas Whangdoodle" that has a little cluster of bright orange plastic eggs and a fringe that wiggles.

With my old rod, some new line . . . ?

Well, as I said, I'm thinking about it.

When the pelicans circle closer and closer to shore, diving repeatedly, its a good sign the surf fish are running. Gulls are all over the place, too, stealing and squabbling.

Local fishermen get out their waders and hand nets and gather along the beach. A hand net is simply a large triangle of netting attached to a couple of sturdy poles. The fisherman grabs the poles at the narrow end and thrusts the wide end of the net into an incoming wave. If he's lucky, he'll catch anything from a half dozen to two dozen fish.

There are two kinds. *Day* surf fish run about six inches long and look something like small trout. You cut off the heads, clean out the small gut cavities and fry them, with or without a coating of corn meal. They each weigh a couple of ounces, more or less; the bones come out easily; you eat until your eyes start to bulge. They're delicious.

Night surf fish are much smaller. You don't bother to clean them at all. Just wash, deep fry and crunch away happily, eating bones, head, tail and all. They have a slightly more oily taste.

When the run is a good one, there's plenty to go around. Bring a small bucket to the beach, and a fisherman will fill it for you and wade out for more.

It isn't as easy as it may sound. Sometimes the net comes up empty more often than not. The surf is cold and dangerous. One of the cardinal rules is never to turn your back on the ocean. Even in calm weather, a sleeper wave can suddenly boom in and wash a netter out into deep water. It's a good idea to fish in groups rather than alone.

One fisherman relates a story about catching night fish. He built

Netting surf fish.

a nice fire and nipped away at a jug of wine until the sun set. Then he started fishing. Naturally, he'd pause now and then to enjoy the warmth of the jug and the fire. Out in the surf, he was suddenly knocked flat by a huge wave. The net was torn from his hands. He struggled to his feet, waist deep, bruised and battered. It was completely black. The wave had put out his fire. He couldn't even tell which way to go to reach the beach. It was a thoroughly frightening few minutes.

Did it teach him a lesson?

"Well, now when I go down to the beach with a jug of wine and build a fire, I don't fish."

One day when I'd scrounged a bucket of silvery day fish during a good run, I stopped at the top of the bluff to talk to a neighbor. He looked at what I was carrying and shuddered.

"What's the matter?" I asked. "Don't you like surf fish?"

"Not any more."

"Golly, I think they're great."

It was obvious he didn't agree. Finally he said, "When I first came up here, I had a net and fished all the time. What we didn't eat, we'd freeze. But one time I came home with a gunnysack full. I started cutting off the heads and cleaning them. It isn't very hard to do, you know. But I had a *lot* of fish. Pretty soon I began to notice that the pile of heads was getting bigger and bigger. I didn't pay much attention at first. Then, suddenly, there seemed to be *thousands of little heads*, and all those eyes were staring at me. It just got to me. I haven't been able to put a net in the water since."

"Look," I said, "I'll clean some for you if you'd like."

"No *thanks*," he said firmly, "Not on your life."

I'm not exactly glad he told me that story.

You might think it would be easy to buy fresh fish most anywhere along the coast. Not so. We have to drive to Bodega Bay south or Noyo north. In either case, it's a round trip of about a hundred miles.

Salmon boats do put in at Point Arena during the summer, but their catch is put on ice and shipped out immediatly. We can watch but not buy.

I suppose the thinking is that anyone too stupid to catch his own fish doesn't deserve any consideration.

And . . . I suppose they're right.

IF YOU FIND
LIFE AMUSING

Some years ago I drove across the Tamar River into Cornwall and stopped at the first pub I could find. I wanted to check out the local ale; I wanted a pasty, that unelegant but delicious meat, potato and onion turnover the Cornish are famous for, and I wanted to unwind.

I'd been driving for five hours, forcing myself to stay on the left hand side of the road, and needed a break. I was also a bit concerned because I didn't know where I was going to stay that night. Cornwall in August can be pretty well booked up, and I wasn't booked anywhere.

So the ale got first priority. I went to the bar and soon was marveling again at the skill of British brewers. The fellow standing next to me spoke, a rarity in England. He turned out to be a Scotsman, a traveling salesman. We chatted a bit, and then I asked him, "Tell me . . . these bed and breakfast places I see along the road. I've never stayed in one. Are they okay?"

"Well," he said with a small smile, "actually, they're fine . . . if you find life amusing."

It was a remark that still pleases me, and I often remember it with comfort, especially these days when everyone seems to take himself so seriously.

It's a good attitude to have when you live on this coast.

If you come here to escape the rat race of the city or the poodle race of suburbia, you certainly can. But you'll also escape many of their conveniences. Some people who want to "get away from it all" find they miss "it all" when they get here and soon move back.

There are nitties and gritties.

First, it's not an easy place to reach. At Jenner, Highway 1 stops meandering pleasantly along the coast and takes off up the hills, climbing with hairpin turns several hundred feet. Then it snakes along the edge of a gigantic bluff for about ten or twelve miles, giving riders magnificent views and drivers fits.

The two-lane road is good, but it curves constantly and sometimes seems as narrow as the paths the sheep use in their almost vertical pastures. It's a long drop to the sea at this point, scary.

One of the local girls was coming up here with her new boyfriend, a six-foot-two-inch basketball player. He attacked the Jenner grade gamely for a couple of miles in his Volkswagen. Then, pale and shaken, he pulled to the side of the road.

"You drive," he muttered and climbed into the back seat, curled up in fetal position and covered his head with a blanket. It was a short romance.

A dear friend of ours got car sick on this stretch of the road years ago and politely refuses to visit us.

Actually, there are only about fifteen minutes of difficult driving.

When you reach Timber Cove, feeling perhaps a bit like Ronald Colman at the top of the pass above Shangri-La, the worst is over. It's a relatively easy go the rest of the way, along a shoreline that has to be one of the most beautiful in the world.

But the Jenner grade is a reality of living on the south Mendocino coast. It has to be driven on any trips to Santa Rosa or the Bay Area, going and coming. The road probably won't be widened appreciably for a long time to come . . . if ever.

To say that Gualala itself in an utterly charming seaside village — like one in Maine, for example — is to speak with more love than truth. Its big white hotel, built in 1903, and its hillside church, used by both Baptists and Episcopalians, have a lot of character, but the remaining buildings are hardly remarkable. The basics are there (small supermarket, restaurants, bank, post office, beauty parlors, nursery) but it's no place to wander about and enjoy quaint shops, quiet streets, picket fences, flower gardens and shuttered houses with cute little porches. For that you have to go to Mendocino about fifty miles up the coast. There, a lot of restoration has gone on. Shop windows are full of antique glass, pottery and paintings waiting for tourists to come and bring money.

In Gualala there has been very little to restore. Most of the lumber company houses that remain from the old days were not too well built and are now a bit shaky, breezy inside when the wind blows.

But it's a beautiful spot for a town to be in. Some day . . . who knows?

Meanwhile, nobody seems to be pressing hard for anything different. And that's fine.

Most of the residents live off the highway and up in the hills. There are advantages to being there. Away from the ocean the weather is much warmer in the summer. Vegetables can be raised, fruit trees bear, huckleberries and blackberries grow in profusion. Home canning and freezing are a big help in keeping a family well fed.

One slight drawback for some of the ladies who moved up flushed with excitement about returning to the good old days of their grandmothers: once the first dozen jars is packed away in the pantry, there's another dozen to fill . . . and another . . . and another. Home canning is demanding work. That old Del Monte label begins to look pretty good again. One slight drawback for their husbands: the deer are hungry and plentiful, and you have to build an eight-foot fence around your garden.

It's all probably worth it, however.

Our first attempts at growing vegetables hard by the ocean ended almost in disaster. Tomatoes, corn, squash, beans didn't seem to like it (or was it us?) at all. We even had little luck with carrots, beets, radishes or lettuce, although some of our neighbors do fairly well. Broccoli? Now that was different. The small plants we put in grew slowly but steadily. They're now nearly four feet high on thick stalks, and they bear all year long. Artichokes do well, too. Chinese snow peas got along famously, but the deer got fat on most of them.

This year we decided to fool Mother Nature. We filled two large tubs with planter mix, fertilized it generously and planted lettuce, white radishes, beets and carrots. The lettuce and radishes did fine; the beets and carrots went all to tops.

Most of the oldtimers have their freezers well-stocked with rockfish, salmon, steelhead and abalone. There's plenty of venison and even wild pig in them, too. So if you hunt, fish, dive for abalone and grow a large garden, you've got it made. If you don't, you have to plan ahead.

I mentioned earlier that it is hard to buy fish. There is no local butcher shop either. Meat is shipped up to the markets once a week, but the selection is limited pretty much to steak, hamburger, pork chops, ham hocks and pot roast. Twice a week, however, a load of chicken from Santa Rosa arrives, and it is excellent.

The local stores have just about everything you really need, but if you get a sudden hankering for sweetbreads, veal scallops, a leg of lamb or green turtle soup, you won't find them.

Most of us make periodic shopping trips to Santa Rosa or Fort Bragg and stock up on things that are hard to get. A good cold chest comes in mighty handy.

On the other hand, grocery stores (somewhat like the old general

The bookmobile is a popular visitor.

stores) do have a selection of work and outdoor clothing . . . pants, jackets, windbreakers, heavy socks and so on. That's something you won't find in your favorite large supermarket.

The latest trendy things? Not much is here. A few small shops are open. Their stocks are small. Nobody pays much attention to what anybody else wears anyway.

You can always rely on mail-order houses, and there are more in business these days than you might think. A wide variety of catalogs arrive at the Gualala post office, quite a few addressed to my wife. We've had very few disappointments buying by mail, and the companies were prompt in exchanging items or refunding the money.

The movie theater at Point Arena, about thirteen miles up the road, is open weekends. There's a book store in Manchester, about twenty miles away. But we are visited by the bookmobile every other week, and it's a marvelous institution. Cars drive in from all over to wait for it, and many people check out a shopping bag full of books at a time. What you can't find, you can order.

Golf? There's a new and demanding nine hole course at The Sea Ranch. It has no clubhouse facilities yet. If you want to drive fifty miles to Little River, you'll find another nine holes.

Tennis may be taking the country by storm; we've hardly felt its breeze yet. There are very few courts at the moment.

Once, when I was walking down the road, a lady in a station wagon with four kids stopped beside me.

"Isn't there a McDonald's *anywhere* along this coast?" she called.

No there isn't. Nor is there a Jack-in-the-Box or a Colonel Sanders.

It takes a while to get to know a place. I'll share some of my wisdom with you. Here are a few gentle survival hints.

Don't tell everyone where you live. Many people who move up here come to dread summer weekends. They suddenly discover they have more friends than they knew they had. Just about the time good old Jim drives away good old Joe drives up. Don't expect to lose yourself in these boondocks and stay lost.

Don't tell anyone about your favorite mushroom patch. My neighbor said "She was a nice little old lady, big smile, wrinkled face, white fluffy hair. Just moved up. She wanted to know about mushrooms, which were good to eat, where to find them. So I said, 'Come with me. I'll show you.' Mr. Nice Guy. I took her up on the ridge. Now this is a great place I've known about for years. Lots of Boletus Kings. Great. It's just off the road.

"I showed her the mushrooms. It was late in the day, so they'd grown a bit too much. But we picked enough for her dinner. 'See all the little ones?' I said. 'They grow fast. By morning they'll be just right. I'm coming up tomorrow early. That's the time to pick them.'

"She was grateful.

"Next morning I drove up with a basket and met her coming down

64

the hill in her little red car. She didn't even wave to me. When I got there, there wasn't a mushroom in sight.

"And you know, I never did get any out of that patch all winter long."

Don't shake dice for drinks. Once, after I'd lived in New York for a couple of years, I flew back to San Francisco for a meeting. It was winter. The plane landed about eight o'clock in the evening just after a storm had gone through. I checked into the Palace and hurried out onto Montgomery Street. The streets were still wet, the air was fresh and soft, the sky was clear and full of moonlight. There were very few cars. The city seemed almost deserted. It was one of those magical moments you never forget.

I passed a bar and could hear laughter inside. God, it was great to be back where people laughed out loud. I quickened my pace and soon arrived at a place called the "Broker's Club." It had once been a favorite of mine and a lot of other people in advertising. I opened the door and could hear again the lovely sound of dice boxes thudding on the bar, the rattle of the shake, the clatter of the roll across scarred wood.

It had been so long I almost cried.

So I know about shaking dice for drinks . . . or thought I did until I moved to Gualala.

In San Francisco, the game is usually Boss Dice, and it's relatively simple. You shake for the best poker hand with five dice. Aces are not wild as they are in some games. Each player has two rolls. The first decides who is boss. If I have a pair of sixes and you have three deuces, you're the boss. You can then leave your deuces on the bar, roll the remaining two dice (this time not revealing them) and decide whether or not you want me to come up . . . that is, take my second roll. If you haven't improved your hand, you may decide not to call me up (that's the advantage of being boss) and the game starts all over again. If you have improved, shaken another deuce, for example, or a pair of anything to give you a full house, you say, "Come up," and I have to shake again. Whoever has the best hand wins. The final winner must win two out of three games.

Clear? Probably not, but you get the idea.

In Gualala, things are different. Each player shakes one die first. The winner can call any game he wants. Say your six has beaten his four. You shake the dice, not revealing your hand. You then call the game. "Boss dice," you say, the old familiar. But your opponent has the right to refuse to play Boss Dice. You then have to call *another* game. "Liar's Dice," you may say, and your adversary, with three aces, eventually beats you.

Simple? Of course it isn't, but that's not all.

Any one of twenty or more games can be called. These include Razzle, Tensy (high or low, two or four) Big Red, Pair, Treys Away, Chinaman (high, middle or low), Hair, Monterey, Chinese Treys Away, Ship-Captain-Crew, our old friends Boss and Liar's and some others.

You can see how the whole thing can get pretty complicated.

On second thought, it really hasn't been complicated at all. I just pay for the drinks and forget about it.

Don't split wood when it's nice and dry. Whaddya mean. That's the best time, isn't it? Nope. The sooner you can split a log after it's cut the better. That dry stuff can be murder.

Don't walk along the edge of a cliff. This one is really important. Sometimes, when people are full of poetry and at one with the sea, they have walked to the top of a cliff and never come back. Just because grass is growing doesn't mean there's solid footing underneath. The grass often grows a foot or so beyond the edge of a cliff. Check first. Then compose your sonnet.

Don't turn your back on the ocean. The only reason I repeat this is that it's easy to forget when you're out there studying the tide pools or contemplating kelp. If a big wave comes in unexpectedly, you might get a better view of undersea marvels than you bargained for.

66

Don't miss the local barbecues. A wild pig or a lamb wrapped in foil and wet gunnysacks and buried with hot rocks—cooked almost Hawaiian style—is out of this world. You can enjoy these feasts a number of times during the year when organizations raise money. Go.

Don't rob a bank. The roads are few, narrow and easily blocked off. There are no alleys to screech into, TV style. By the time you swerve around a couple of slow-moving campers the sheriff will be waiting for you or his helicopter will be chopping away over your head.

Don't worry about what to wear. Pack your Gucci's away and buy work shoes and a pair of rubber boots. It's trendy to be practical anyway. The only time suits are worn is at funerals.

Don't pay any attention to deer crossing signs. Decide once and for all that deer will cross *anyplace.* They're plentiful, especially early in the morning and evenings. When one darts in front of your car, there's almost sure to be another following. Hitting a deer is not recommended. Nobody wins.

Don't trust your compass. There are iron deposits between Gualala and Anchor Bay that raise hob with the needle. You won't really want to know exactly where you are anyway.

Don't expect a perfect television picture. The Sea Ranch and Point Arena have cables. Other places the reception varies. It's generally good along the shore. Behind hills, of course, you may have trouble. The best reception comes at times when it's cloudy or foggy in San Francisco. I suppose the signal bounces more favorably.

Don't worry about earthquakes. It won't do you much good. There are enough faults for everyone under the area. It does pay, I think, to build a bit more solidly than you might other places. If the big one comes, be prepared to take a deep breath and start swimming.

67

Don't tell anyone about your favorite huckleberry patch. See mushroom section above.

Don't let beauty blind you. The lot you may want to buy may be perfectly lovely, but make certain you can get water there and that the soil percolates sufficiently for a septic system before you sign the papers. Much of the land was formed when old beaches raised, and there is a hard rock pan close to the surface.

Don't rely on San Francisco weather reports. When a storm threatens the city, it can already be raining here. When gutters are ankle-deep along Market Street, the sun can be shining in Gualala.

Don't feed the racoons. Be firm the first time they appear at your door or on your patio. You know they've come for food. They know they've come for food. If they don't get it in two or three visits, they'll go someplace else more accommodating. Of course, you'll feel like Scrooge and wake up from dreams of those intelligent, accusing eyes. But don't give in. Once you do, they've got you.

Do feed the racoons. After all, racoons are delightful, and they're far less trouble than having a dog or any other pet. You'll look forward to their nightly visits. Your guests will find them an amusing diversion. Eventually, the first pair you feed will be back with another generation . . . then another and another. You'll be buying kibble in 10-pound sacks. But that shouldn't matter. It's only dog food.

Don't get your dander up. You might stunt the growth of your potted plants.

GETTING THINGS DONE

Along the New England coast and many other places in the East it may take as long as a generation for a new family to be truly accepted into the community.

The old families run things, stick together and are only reluctantly tolerant of Johnny-come-latelies, sometimes hardly even civil.

Here, you can be asked to serve on a committee almost before your pots and pans are unpacked.

One of our new friends remarked about it a bit ruefully the other day. "You know," he said, "I came up here to retire and paint, and right at this moment I have eight community projects I'm working on. Eight. I'm busy all the time."

Part of the reason, of course, is that the really old families are out-numbered. Not too long ago there were only a few ranches along a hundred miles of coast. If any of these families (those that are still here) want to remain aloof, deplore the influx of strangers and remember the good old days, they can. But they don't make anyone feel unwelcome because nobody knows he's being snooted.

Most of the people who live here today have come in the last ten or fifteen years. They share a love of the area, a very real sense of community and, I think, a sense of common adventure.

We're all in this boat together is the feeling, somewhat the way it was in the towns of the old West when they began to grow.

Pioneers? Well, hardly . . . but almost.

We have no local government in Gualala . . . no mayor, no council, no political camps. Nobody has his hand in the till. There is no till.

Ukiah, the county seat, is ninety miles away over some steep mountains on winding roads. I doubt that the county fathers pay much attention to Gualala, certainly no more than they have to.

And this isn't bad at all. We're spared a lot of squabble, back-biting and inflated blood pressure readings.

Of course, we pay taxes for and get some county services. There are sheriff's deputies on patrol and on call. Schools are shared; school buses run. Roads are repaired. We get some help in buying fire equipment. Building permits are issued, inspectors inspect.

Anything else that seems desirable or necessary people get together and do.

The system works rather well.

About twenty years ago it was decided the town needed a community center, a place to hold meetings, put on shows, dances or whatever.

So everybody pitched in and built one.

The lumber company contributed the land and a good share of the materials. The work was done by volunteers. Later, some major additons were made. The main building now includes a 40 by 70 foot hall, a large fully-equipped kitchen, a stage with curtains and dressing rooms, a fireplace, toilets. There is a smaller secondary building, a parking area and a flagpole.

Nobody remembers what the original center cost in terms of cash. Probably not a whole lot. The additions came to thirteen thousand five hundred dollars.

That's about what it takes in San Francisco today to fund a committee to study the feasibility of making a feasibility study.

Lincoln Center it is not, but it works.

How does it support itself?

Top: where all the action is: Community Center.

Left: Ole Wilson, one of the original builders of the Community Center.

It has to pay its taxes of course and its bills for upkeep, cleaning, repairs, electricity, water, insurance and anything else. The Community Center Association manages its affairs and raises some money by a small membership fee. When it is rented, the charge is twelve and a half dollars a night, hardly a whopping sum.

Most of the money needed comes from a monthly Pay 'n Take Sale. People donate used clothing, appliances, cribs, toys, dishes, tools, books, sports equipment . . . just about anything. The prices charged are very low, and this is a real help to many families who live where jobs are few and often available on a seasonal basis.

A Steelhead Derby provides the other major source of income. Tickets are sold; anglers who catch the biggest fish win prizes; there is a banquet at the end of the season.

The benefits of this do-it-yourself operation are both social and practical. The facility is available whenever it's needed. Those who do the work have the satisfaction of making a real contribution to the community. The Pay 'n Take Sale fills a genuine need. The fishermen and their neighbors have a lot of fun.

And nobody owes anybody anything.

I'll never forget a photograph of my father taken about 1900. He was wearing a track suit cut off just above the knees. He was half-crouched and holding the shaft of a high-wheeled hose cart along with seven other runners. They all looked grimly determined. They were the fastest volunteer firemen in his town in Northern Michigan and they often held competitions with their brethren from neighboring communities.

In races down Main Street, they would pull the cart for a hundred yards. Then one of the team—the biggest—would drop back, grab the end of the hose, stick his heels in the ground and hold on until it unwound.

"All of a sudden it was like running in sand up to your knees," my father used to tell me. I enjoyed hearing the stories again and again. He didn't seem to mind telling them either.

In my father's day, volunteer firemen were talked-about heroes. They marched in parades, sat at head tables, entertained visiting firemen lavishly. In Gualala today, the volunteer firemen keep a relatively low profile, but they're there, and they do a surprisingly good job.

"About seven of us started back in 1954," the chief told me. He runs one of the local gas stations. "It was strictly volunteer. We held dances, raised some money and bought shovels and burlap bags we could wet and use to slap out brush fires. Then, a few years later, we became a fire district and could get help from the county buying equipment. It's still all volunteer as far as the men are concerned. There are fifteen now. We're covered by insurance in case we get hurt, but we don't get a dime otherwise."

"What kind of equipment do you have now?"

"Three tankers, three pumpers and a first aid van. One of the pumpers and a tanker are kept in town, another pair at Anchor Bay and the third up on the ridge."

"That's a lot of territory to cover. How do you get the men together if there's a fire."

"We've developed a pretty good system. In fact, people have written us from other parts of the country to find out how it works. We had the phone company install twelve special telephones in the homes of volunteers. When someone calls the fire number, all twelve ring at the same time. Somebody's sure to be around. If a man is out working, his wife knows where to find him. He just drops everything and gets there as fast as possible. Usually . . . say anywhere around town here . . . we can have some of the guys at the fire and working in three to five minutes. Takes longer up in the hills, of course. But we all move, and we know what we're doing."

"What if you need help?"

"We have mutual aid agreements with The Sea Ranch, Point Arena and the military base there. And the forestry people come in to keep fires from spreading. That's always the big worry when there are a lot of trees and brush. We want to keep any fire that starts contained."

So do I, heaven knows.

The same group functions as a rescue team, and it's needed three or four times a month. Often the problem is a heart attack. There are a number of older people who have retired here. Eight of the volunteers have taken training (similar to that given paramedics) that rates them as Emergency Medical Technicians. They know what to do.

They also know what to do when visitors refuse to believe that the cliffs, waves and tides can be dangerous, although it is frequently too late. They've saved many who were stranded on rocks, unable to move part way down a bluff, or washed out by an undertow. But they have been far from totally successful.

That ocean can be meaner than it looks.

All the rescue equipment—resuscitators, aspirators, wet suits, ropes, climbing gear and the newest trauma kit—is carried in a new van. In the community tradition, it was contributed by the Lion's Club whose members cut and sold more than three hundred loads of firewood to raise the money. The wood? Yes, that was donated, too.

Art-in-the-Redwoods is one of the major events of the year. Lunch is provided and a lot of people help.

The turkey lady called first.

"Will you cook a turkey for the show?"

"Of course," said my wife. "How big a turkey should we order?"

"No, we buy them. You just pick one up at the market, roast it, carve it and bring it down. Anything left you keep."

"Fine," said my wife. "My husband will be glad to carve it."

It's a job I detest.

Almost immediately the phone rang again. This time it was the meat loaf lady. "Will you bake a meat loaf for the show?"

"We'd be happy to," my wife said. "We're going to roast a turkey. Does that matter?"

Silence. I gathered that no one was being asked to do more than one cooking job.

"Well, okay. We'll do the turkey then."

"Hey, why didn't you make a switch? I'm great at carving meat loaf."

Hardly the hint of a smile.

Two days later the potato salad lady called. This time I answered.

"I remember the marvelous potato salad your wife brought last year. I wonder if she'd make another for the show?"

"She'd love to," I said. "She does make good potato salad, doesn't she. We're supposed to cook a turkey, but maybe something could be arranged . . . ?"

"Oh blast, I knew I shouldn't have gone out of town. No, that will be all right. I'll manage."

"Well, if you run into any trouble, let us know. She loves to make potato salad."

I'm not above lying in a good cause either.

These, of course, are minor matters. Putting on an art show calls for a great deal of effort and skill. Altogether, about two hundred people work on Art-in-the-Redwoods, some of them for months. Entry forms have to be printed and distributed. Plants have to be potted, watered and cared for. Publicity has to be written, a judge selected and contacted. The material has to be checked in and usually arrives on the last possible day. Then it must be separated into groups and judged. (This year, two hundred and seven entries were received, including works in oil, water color, acrylic, pencil, collage, silkscreen, photography, woodcut, weaving, clay, stitchery, stoneware, ceramics, steel, macrame, ink, batik, pastel, wood, stained glass and yarn and foam. Pick your medium; have at it.) Finally, in a frantic flurry, the show has to be hung to look its best.

Each year, a special lattice-roofed terrace is constructed for an outside dining area and decorated with redwood boughs. Shelves are built for plant display. The kitchen is manned (or personed). Tables are set up and ticket sellers are given full change boxes. A program, of course, is printed.

We drove up the coast to pick up entries of artists who had no way of getting them to the show, a small contribution compared to that of many others.

On the day Art-in-the-Redwoods opened my wife had to make an unexpected trip to Santa Rosa. I cooked the turkey, carved and delivered it.

Next year I'm going to call the meat loaf lady early.

It would be wrong to leave the impression that everyone who lives here spends all his time rushing around doing good. Projects have to be sold and believed in. Sometimes this is difficult. Once something does get started, work has to be scheduled and the willing workers reminded constantly of their willingness.

"The first weekend we started putting siding on the firehouse up on the ridge, there were so many hammers going it was dangerous to be near the place," one of the old hands told me. "The next weekend nobody showed up."

Eventually, everything works out . . . and rather well.

"Eventually" is a good word to remember, for there is another side to the problem of getting things done—getting them done for you.

Yesterday I called the plumber.

"Tom, got a problem. My toilet keeps running. It flushes all right, but when it fills up it doesn't stop. I think there's something wrong with the ballcock." This last to show I knew a thing or two.

"Keeps running, does it? Got a rope?"

"A *rope*?"

"Just tie it down. That'll keep it from running until I can get there."

I was surprised when he showed up a couple of hours later. He's a hard man to pin down. Seems to have a lot of projects going at the same time. He has bushy blond eyebrows, bright blue eyes and a round craggy face. He always wears a wool stocking cap and a heavy knitted sweater that tightly encases a big chest and a fair amount of belly. He and his wife are much loved around our town, but he's been known to be firm with newcomers.

A lady once called him about dinnertime. "That little pipe that brings the water to the toilet has broken. I've had to shut it off, and I have eight people here for the weekend. Will you please come and fix it?"

"Don't make night calls," said Tom.

"But what am I going to do? *Eight* people!"

"You've got water in the kitchen?"

"Yes."

"You've got a pail?"

"Yes."

"Well, just give everybody who wants to use the toilet a pail of water to carry in with them. That'll work fine."

But, as I say, he arrived promptly at my house, took the cover off the offending toilet, flushed it and stared into the depths while it filled.

"One of those damned plastic things," he muttered, fiddling with the ballcock plunger. "Got a crescent wrench?"

"Hey," I said. "That's the oldest gag there is. You mean you've forgotten your tools?"

"Naw," he said, grinning. "They're in the other truck. My son took it this morning."

I found a pliers and the only wrench I had. Both were too small. Tom went out to his truck and came back immediately with a big wrench and a huge pliers. He also had a small cellophane bag. "I even found a replacement," he said. "We'll put a new one in."

This time he was able to work the ballcock gizmo loose. It was a simple thing—washer on top, plunger through the middle, washer on the bottom.

Tom picked up the bag containing the replacement and looked at it for a long moment, obviously puzzled.

"Can you imagine?" he said. "They didn't include the second washer. There's only one in there."

He pushed the plunger up and down, inspected the two used washers, wiped them clean.

"Must have been some gunk caught in there," he said and put the old ballcock back together again. He flushed the toilet, and this time it worked properly.

"Fixed," he said. "Can you imagine those guys . . . only one washer?"

This morning the toilet started running again.

I've tied it down with a good strong rope.

I'll call Tom . . . as soon as I'm sure he's had breakfast, of course.

I'm certain the toilet will be fixed. I'm not sure exactly when. Tom's a good man (a history buff, by the way, who specializes in the First World War), but he has a lot of territory to cover, actually miles of it. And this is true of almost anyone who can repair anything.

Our chimney was originally capped with a sheetmetal cover. It was much too flimsy. The galvanized iron began to disintegrate in a couple of years. Whenever the wind blew, large flecks of rusty metal landed on our deck, a constant reminder that salt air may be lovely to breathe, but it's tough on iron.

(I just looked at that sentence with growing apprehension. We all brag about having the cleanest air in America. Has anyone ever found out what happens to rats when they breathe salt air? I don't think I want to know.)

The nearest sheetmetal shop is in Fort Bragg. The guy agreed to drop in the next time he had a job down the coast, and, a month later, he arrived, took measurements and recommended a copper cover, considerably more expensive than the original.

"Copper's best out here," he said, nodding toward the ocean and spitting off the deck.

"Okay," I said. "When?"

"I get down here fairly often," he said reasonably enough. "You don't want to pay for a special trip, do you?"

"Not if I don't have to, but I don't want rain coming down into the fireplace."

"I'll be in touch."

I called him a month later. He hesitated for a long moment. "Yeah, now I remember. I've got those measurements somewhere. Just haven't had anything to do down there."

The rains were due soon, but, with luck, things would probably be all right for a while.

"Well, make it as soon as you can."

"I'll be in touch. What was your number again? Better give it to me so I'm sure I have it."

I never did hear from him again, nor could I reach him. Maybe he went out of business. Nothing terrible happened. It was the driest winter in years. But this year I've got to get something done. I'm starting in July. I figure I should be able to get a new cap put on by the first of October.

That's my target date anyway.

To be fair, there are a lot of people around who can do many things, and—if the steelhead aren't running or the deer season isn't open—they're perfectly happy to help you out. They work hard, and their rates are not anywhere near the horrendous charges that are made in the Bay Area. You just have to plan ahead, be patient.

The best place to find out about them is at the hotel bar late in the afternoon. That's Miller time, as the advertising claims, and it seems to be true here. Miller beer is a big seller.

"Know anybody who can take down some big, dead branches in my bull pines?"

"How tall?"

"The trees? Maybe eighty feet. Too big for me."

Thoughtful pause. Call down the bar. "Hey, who's that guy lives up on the ridge road with the spikes and belts for climbing trees?"

Somebody shouts a name.

"Yeah, that's the guy. He can go up anything. He's in the book."

I called him and made a date. He arrived only three days after he said he would, looked up at the trees briefly and began strapping on his spikes. He had one long rope for himself, another for his chain saw. These he tossed over a strong limb and began climbing. Branches began crashing down. He moved around in the trees like a rock climber, made it look like fun. I kept wondering if my insurance really covered accidents.

In a little more than an hour, he had the dead stuff cleared out and the wood cut up for the fireplace. It was not a small job. He charged me about what I'd once paid a plumber in San Rafael who spent ten minutes cleaning out a clogged disposal unit.

Of course I had to pile the wood myself. I've learned how to do that. The best way is one piece at a time.

Some of our neighbors are constantly annoyed by what they call the "Gualala *Mañana* Attitude." I'm afraid there are only two things they can do. The most sensible is to learn how to do the work themselves. The other is to hang a bosun's chair from the ceiling. Then, at least, when they climb the walls, they can enjoy the view.

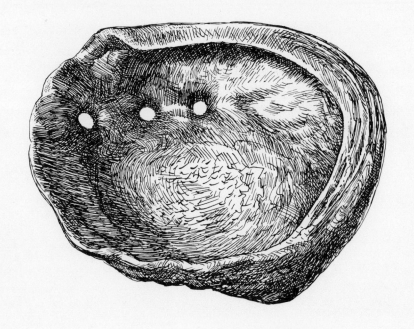

ABALONE FEVER

When, in my innocence, I first moved to the coast, I was pleased and astonished at how popular it was on weekends. Highway 1 would often be lined with cars and trailers parked anywhere there was room.

"How nice," I thought. "People really do enjoy the beauties of nature . . . the trees, the cliffs, the birds, the waves."

It was, in a way, a justification of my own feelings.

I was even more impressed when I saw that many of the visitors had wet suits. They must, I was sure, want to study the undersea life like Jacques Cousteau. Marvelous.

I knew nothing about abalone fever.

It's a disease that infects thousands of divers who descend on us

An abalone diver heads for deep water.

from all over the state whenever there's a series of minus tides—that is, tides considerably lower than average. Motels and campgrounds fill up, trailer parks are jammed, and those who can't find a place to stay sleep in their cars.

A game warden told me that during one period of extremely low tides fifty thousand people arrived, and the coast—in terms of abalone, at least—has never quite recovered. Estimates for other weekends vary from four to ten thousand visitors. Not all go in the water, but a lot of abalone gets packed away. And why not? It's almost impossible to find on the market any more, and, when you can, it costs ten or twelve dollars a pound.

I dug into the story and found that indeed the abalones are being seriously depleted. Not too many years ago it was possible to find the huge mollusks on rocks revealed when the tide went out, pry them off with a tire iron and be in business. This was called abalone "picking," and it has virtually ceased to exist except in rare coves privately owned and almost inaccessible.

Now, to capture the wily ab, you have to get wet, and with a wet suit you can.

The problem is that abalones exist in a rather narrow band along the shore usually to a depth of about thirty-five feet — unlike those in Southern California waters as deep as seventy feet where they can logically be commercially harvested. Thus, the abalones in our area are all within two or three hundred feet offshore, well within reach of the hunters in their wet suits.

To be fair, getting your limit is not easy even when you're snugly suited up. It depends on how skillful you are at free diving (air tanks are illegal) and how lucky you are at finding untouched areas on the ocean floor. These are diminishing where there is easy access to the shoreline. It is almost as if the depleted areas spread out from the beaches like the splayed fingers of your hand.

Of course, much of the coastline is rugged and protected by steep cliffs, but man has always been an ingenious hunter. Now, on calm days, boats, rubber rafts, surfboards and even canoes are used to get to previously hard-to-reach places.

All this, naturally, makes abalone hunting a sport to many people, and perhaps it should be looked at in that way. But there are arguments that disagree. Some believe that abalone fever is much the same as that which infected the gold prospectors. There's something terribly exciting about striking it rich, but is it sport? The abalone can't move, can't elude its pursuer, is not taken on a skillfully cast fly or even shot on the wing. It's a creature cursed by having an expensive and mighty delicious foot that can't carry it an inch away from danger.

The female abalone lays about a million to a million and a half eggs. Most become fish food. Those that are fertilized hatch into larvae. Without shells, the larvae float freely in the water for ten days, much to the delight of hungry rockfish, plankton, starfish and crabs. When their shells begin to form, those few that have escaped settle to the ocean floor and will live *if* they land on a smooth rock and near food they can eat, single-celled diatons and algae. Two have to survive to perpetuate the species. The average score is not much better than that.

An abalone grows about an inch a year for the first three years; then the rate slows to half an inch and diminishes still more after it reaches seven inches. The largest red abalone, the kind most prevalent in our waters, ever recorded measured just under twelve inches.

So the diver who takes a legal-sized abalone (one measuring seven inches or more) brings to a close a chapter of undersea life that has taken at least a dozen years to write.

I mention legal-sized, for there are strict laws. Each hunter is now allowed four abalones, and he must take them himself. When, as often happens, Joe in his wet suit goes down to the rocks with his wife and two kids and fills a bag for each member of the family, he's in big trouble . . . if he gets caught. This is called "party picking" and it's a no-no, but a lot of people try to get away with it and all too often succeed.

It's difficult at a camp site to prove that ma and the kids didn't pry off their own limit, so wardens have developed several methods of control. One is to park on the beach in full uniform and in official cars and check divers as they come in. This seems to have a deterrent effect. Not many violations are found. Wardens also watch the coves from bluffs using powerful binoculars. When they see evidence of party picking (sometimes, the wardens say, it's almost like watching an assembly line in action) they move in and make their arrests. The most effective method is to work undercover, that is, arrive in unmarked cars, wear wet suits and join the hunters.

Recently, over a three-day weekend, forty-one arrests were made using this technique.

Violators must appear in court and are now judged severely. One was recently fined $435.00 for possessing twelve more than his limit.

The boom is really lowered if people are caught taking abalone for commercial sale. Two men were picked up near Elk with eighty-nine in possession. One received a ten-month sentence, the other, on parole, was sent back to Federal prison. Two commercial fishermen landed in

San Francisco with six hundred saying they were taken off the Farallones where it is legal to hunt for sale. They had been observed gathering their catch off Point Reyes. They lost their boat; one was fined twenty-five hundred dollars, the other fifteen hundred dollars. Both were prohibited from fishing for three years.

There is another problem. Until recently, it was believed that returning an undersized abalone to its rock was a reasonable assurance it would continue to live and grow. A test was made. A group with cut feet, injuries similar to those often made by the irons hunters use, were put in a tank. A similar group, uninjured, were put in a second tank. Fifty-eight percent of the injured mollusks died. It was discovered that their "blood" coagulates extremely slowly. Only one of the uninjured abalones died during the test.

Usually, even a careful hunter will return several undersized abalones in reaching his limit. Their mortality rate must be extremely high.

I wrote an article about this for *California Living* (substantially the same material included here), and it got a lot of reaction, not all favorable.

One angry wet-suiter wrote:

> While acknowledging success at diving takes skill, Verran questions whether it is a sport, because the ab can't elude his pursuer. By the time one has submerged twenty or thirty feet without air tanks and searched through murky water, rocks and kelp, there is often not enough bottom time for the diver to attempt prying an ab from a rock, assuming he's lucky enough to see one. Although the ab can't run from danger, the author neglects to mention it can exert a vicelike grip. I'm often unable to pry an ab iron between the ab's protective shell and the rock to which it's attached.

My intention wasn't to hurt anyone's feelings. If doing something that uncomfortable and dangerous makes it a sport, it's okay with me. The difficulties he describes, however, really support the major point.

Not too long ago a twelve-year-old child could wade out in tennis shoes and get his abalone. Now a strong man has to dive twenty or thirty feet to find one. If so many hadn't been taken, would this be necessary?

Another reader wrote:

> ...a very important contributor to the demise of this shoreline delicacy was overlooked — the sea otter. The divers Verran describes may be contributors, but it's not likely they are the main cause of the abalone abolition.

Now it's perfectly true that sea otters eat abalone. They also eat sea urchins, crabs, snails, mussels, scallops, squid, barnacles, octopus, starfish arms and even certain fishes. They're lovely little creatures, but they also get hungry.

It would be nice for our friends in wet suits to say that the sea otters are to blame.

The trouble is, there are no sea otters along the Marin, Sonoma or Mendocino coasts. They all live down around Monterey Bay. The depletion of the abalone population in this area has to be caused by man.

Other divers wrote that bat rays and fish are the real culprits. They report that often when they're hunting there's a swarm of predators around them. Bat rays have even been known to snatch a bag of abalones away from a diver. Why not? The hard work, prying the abs off, has already been done. The diver has done it.

When an undersized abalone is replaced by a diver, it's highly vulnerable to any hungry fish before it gets a chance to clamp down ... if it can. Sheepshead, cabazone, starfish, and octopus are known to eat the mollusk, but they're not considered to be a serious menace.

Finding other culprits doesn't help much. Man, with the wet suit, can now range over most of the abalone's growing area, and he should recognize his impact.

I'm not for taking away anyone's pleasure or sport. If some kind soul gives me an abalone, I'll prepare and eat it with great enjoyment. I know the Fish and Game people are dedicated and are watching the situation carefully. The season was shortened recently, for example.

What really bothers me is this. There are a lot of greedy divers who rip-off the coast. (In this case, the new expression "rip-off" couldn't possibly be more precise!) We hear about them all the time.

A couple from Sacramento brags about having five hundred pounds in their freezer. Abalone doesn't freeze too well and is not exactly great after a few months. The newspapers report that much, taken supposedly for sport, is being sold illegally to restaurants. There are stories of divers who have false bottoms in water pails and coolers and of others who stash away large catches in sea caves, returning at night to retrieve them.

There are many miles of coastline, and it's almost impossible to police it all.

I know it is unfair to condemn a group for the actions of a few. Most divers probably obey the law and are aware of the problem. But every time I see a group of wet-suited figures moving down the trail to a beach I can't help being reminded of the arrival of buffalo hunters on the Western plains.

MAKING A BUCK

The economic tide has ebbed and flowed a number of times along the coast since it first opened to settlers in the early eighteen sixties.

It's probably gently on the flow again after several years of coast protection limitations on building. Still, I doubt that this is a place to come to hoping to get rich rapidly . . . yet anyway.

There are some family businesses—grocery stores, gas stations, lumber yards, restaurants—that manage to provide a reasonably good living. Construction workers keep busy, part of the year at least. Anybody who can fix appliances or anything else is in demand. But if you want to sell professional services, think twice. The few doctors and dentists who have served here haven't come close to matching the income they could make other places. Some have left, regretfully, and sometimes haven't been replaced for a long time. There are not many lawyers.

If you're a CPA, for example, and want to retire working part-time, you might find some bookkeeping chores to do, but that's about all.

On the other hand, a veterinarian recently opened shop and within a couple of months had four hundred patient cards in his file. His services had long been needed.

This is still pretty much rural country. The first homestead rights were grants of one hundred eighty and three hundred sixty acres. The initial commercial crop was apples. They were dried, skidded down the hills, loaded on boats and shipped to San Francisco. Later potatoes and peas were grown. They were of excellent quality, according to reports. There were also fields of oats, barley and wheat.

All these ventures suffered from one problem—remoteness.

In the early days, it took two days to get from the Russian River to Gualala. Even as late as the nineteen forties Highway 1 was a dirt road, and there were eighteen gates to open and shut on your trip. This made it tough to get crops to market profitably.

Ranches now mostly run dairy herds and sheep. The dairy farmers have to meet much more stringent regulations than they once did. Taxes have increased. Markets are still a long way off. As for sheep, well, it takes three acres to support a ewe; a lamb sells for about twelve dollars; the wool market has been off for a number of years. Money making opportunities in either case are not too great.

Through most of the years (but not all by any means) logging was a great source of income for many and made a few wealthy. When the virgin redwoods were being removed in the eighteen eighties, times were very good. It was then that the huge logs were dragged out of the forests by oxen, dinky railroads and stationary engines winding in spools of wire rope. Just about every gulch had its mill, and lumber was loaded onto ships by sliding it down chutes. The vessels, called the

90

"Swedish Navy" because many of the sailors were Scandinavian, anchored perilously close to the cliffs in "dog holes."

Tanbark and railroad ties were the principal products shipped out. A lot of the coast's lumber was used to rebuild San Francisco when it burned down several times.

During the early nineteen hundreds and even up through the forties, the Mendocino coast was enisled beyond time and almost everything else. Those who lived here had to be extremely self-sufficient. Visiting the area was an adventure that only a few enjoyed.

With the coming of the postwar building boom, the lumbering business opened up again. A number of people who had been farsighted enough to buy land at a dollar and a half an acre sold their timber rights and did just fine, thank you. There were eighteen mills in the Gualala vicinity alone. By then, Highway 1 had been paved. Logs and lumber could be trucked out.

"It was a wonderful time," one ex-lumberjack told me. "Everybody had a pocketful of money and no place to spend it."

The fifties are still remembered with affection.

The mills began to close down one by one about 1960, the last in 1969. Whatever trees are cut now are hauled somewhere else for milling.

About this time a new source of employment opened up. The Ohlson ranch which ran for ten miles along the north Sonoma coast was purchased for three and a half million dollars. Castle and Cook was the buyer. A development of retirement and second homes was started called The Sea Ranch.

Those who were losing their jobs with the closing of the mills could find work again. Roads had to be put in, drainage systems built, electric lines installed underground, lots cleared and, later, houses constructed. The transition was a smooth one, and the economy didn't suffer much from the passing of the lumbering business. At the moment, however, new building is being kept to a minimum.

What about good old American enterprise? Can't someone with a good idea succeed on the coast? Yes, but it is not easy. For example:

St. Orres

About half way between Gualala and Anchor Bay is a large, heavy-timbered building with two towers capped by copper-covered, onion-shaped domes.

It looks much like an old Russian church, or perhaps a house from a Gothic romance novel. Or, one could think, it was built by some wealthy, eccentric lumber baron years ago.

It is none of these. The building is new; the romance is current, and the builders are young people who have banded together to make a dream come true.

In 1972, Eric, Richard, Bob, and an attorney, who has since been bought out, purchased the old Seaside Hotel and twenty-eight acres of land plus access to a beach . . . that is, they made the necessary down payment. Their idea was not to restore the building but to gut it, use what they could and build an inn that would reflect the character of the region. It would be Russian in motif, harking back to the days of the first colonists.

They would do most of the work themselves and would make no compromises in the quality of its construction. The inn would be built of sturdy timbers. The siding would be thick cedar. There would be double walls completely insulated. Doors would be solid oak with stained glass.

It would, in short, be a creative and artistic venture as well as one that—possibly in time—could make money.

"We wanted," said Eric, "to be able to look at what we built and be proud to say we did it."

Eric had been a carpenter, a foreman and a construction superintendent in the Bay Area. Richard had been a road manager for music groups. Bob was also a carpenter. They were all about thirty years old.

St. Orres, a dream come true.

None had been enchanted with the short-cuts and often shoddy work-manship they had seen.

Their building would be massive, solid, strong.

The name they chose — St. Orres — was not picked for any religious significance. St. Ores had been the family name of an early settler who once owned the land. The creek that bounded the property was called St. Orres with an added "r" on government maps.

They drew up the plans and specifications themselves. After all, they had worked on dozens of buildings and knew what was needed. The county commission turned them down. There was nothing wrong, but the plans had not been drawn by an architect, a designer or an engineer. What fun can a bureaucracy have if it doesn't enforce rules? They had to hire a retired engineer and get his stamp of approval before they were given a final okay.

Meanwhile, they worked on the old hotel and salvaged what they could.

Now they needed timber, especially huge beams to support a structure that would be forty feet high. That kind of material is almost impossible to get these days, and what there is, is frightfully expensive. They found an old mill for sale in Philo that had been built a hundred years ago when wood was plentiful. They bought and dismantled it, trucking the lumber over the mountains to the building site. The inch-thick cedar planks they wanted for siding were discovered in Oregon at a shipbuilder's. They bought his seconds which were much better and less expensive than any commercially available. Other lumber came from Pier 41 in San Francisco and a marvelous sub-floor in an old Manchester barn.

Much of the material had to be cut to proper sizes. Again they did the work themselves with a gas-driven sawmill.

The days went by; their money dwindled; they lived close to poverty levels. In eight months, the outside shell of the inn was up and roofed over, domes and all. But they were broke and deeply in debt.

The attorney had not been able to raise new money . . . at least on terms that seemed reasonable to them. Work had to stop.

Or start in another way.

In a wry gesture of hope, they painted the tarpaper-covered domes with bright yellow stars and moons and went back to the Bay Area to "hustle" for jobs. In two and a half years they paid off debts totaling eighteen thousand dollars and were able to hold onto the property, although the threat of foreclosure hung constantly over their heads.

This was end of the rope time. Bob, with a wife and family to support, could continue no longer. There were offers of money, but accepting them would have meant losing control and being forced to make the compromises they had set out to avoid.

"I know we were lousy businessmen," Eric said, "but it seemed to us there were a lot of sharks out there waiting for us to go under."

Still they did have a building, even though it was far from finished and the yellow moons on its domes had almost faded from sight.

The possibility of selling to Gualala Arts came up and was reluctantly agreed to. After several months of community wrangling, the Arts members voted against the purchase.

If this were a novel written early in the century, you wouldn't expect it to end on such a sad note.

It doesn't.

You also wouldn't expect the author to get out of his predicament by having Eric suddenly receive an unexpected inheritance. That would be a bit too much.

But that's what happened. "Out of the blue" there came enough money to pay off Bob, clear up remaining debts and go ahead.

Eric and Richard went back to work full time. They were joined by others, including our old friends Mike and Cathy. Mike worked on everything from putting in the water and septic systems to designing an arbor, using posts made from logs washed up on the beach. Cathy, in charge of landscaping, dug ditches for sprinkling pipes, planted an herb garden for the kitchen and planned for vegetables. Others taped sheet-rock, painted walls and finished cabinets. Leif, the chef with thirteen years experience, acted as a "go-fer" man, picking up materials and equipment, and also painted. A lady named Samm designed and finished the stained glass used in the doors and the domed towers.

Their hope in the long run is to provide work for a lot of friends who helped when help was needed.

"I guess," Eric said with a grin, "we're not dealing with a piece of land and a building at all. We're dealing in people."

The restaurant was able to open early in 1977. It has a bar and a sitting room with a massive stone and brick fireplace, a large dining room under one of the domes and, of course, a kitchen.

Eight guest rooms were finished about six months later, each designed and built by one of the carpenters, using oak and redwood for most of the furniture. Eventually there will be twenty-four cabins and a gift shop.

Will it all be successful?

In a way it already is. You can now see the lights through the

95

Joanna, the Whale-Watching Editor.

stained glass under the copper-covered domes, and it's a very pretty
sight on a soft misty night. It's nice, too, to hear the sound of music
and laughter when you open the door to go in.

The Independent Coast Observer

An English Lit major fresh out of school, Joanna became the first
copy girl ever to work for the Cincinnati *Times Star*. The editor gave
her the job because there wasn't much else he could do. All the copy
boys had been drafted.

She later became a reporter and was pleased that she never had to
write for the society section. She covered basketball, bowling, general
news and even wrote obits. "But never society," she said with some
satisfaction. Women working on newspapers in those days were usually
stuck with that chore and were not considered real reporters.

Now, some years later, she's Whale Watching Editor, Moon Editor,

Bird Watching Editor, Butterfly Editor and Wildflower Editor of the *Independent Coast Observer.*

She's also its publisher.

The paper, although it headquarters in Gualala, covers the area from Jenner to Point Arena. Since this includes part of Sonoma County as well as part of Mendocino County, she has created a new land called the "Mendonoma Coast." In reality, it's a logical unit in terrain, beauty and common problems. Perhaps the name is not as dramatic as "Costa del Sol" or "Costa Brava" on the Mediterranean, but it serves a purpose.

The ICO, as the paper is called, is extremely well written, bright and lively, and it meets the needs of its readers. If there's going to be a wild pig barbecue in Annapolis, we read about it . . . and want to. If someone has spotted a whale in midsummer, something that rarely happens, we read about it and are amazed. We want to know when the bookmobile will arrive and how long it will stay, when the tides will be high and low, when actors' groups are putting on their shows, when artists are exhibiting, when the dump is open, what the latest rainfall was.

We enjoy seeing pictures of the first irises that lead the wildflower parade in February, or the seals basking on the rocks in winter, or local kids performing in their summer tumbling class.

Front page stories in city dailies are usually full of bad news. The ICO's can be full of mystery.

FOREIGN FISHING BOAT
SIGHTED OFF MENDONOMA

By Barge and Boat Editor

Curious maneuvers of a curious looking ship off the Mendonoma Coast were first brought to the attention of the ICO Barge and Boat Editor last Saturday by Janice Holloway who keeps a sharp eye on the ocean waves while putting permanent ones in her patron's hair at her beauty salon.

A call to retired Sea Captain Clay Hiller of Gualala brought the information that the vessel appeared to be of foreign registry, probably a Japanese or Korean fishing boat, and he estimated it to be about seven miles offshore.

The boat (or is it a ship?) that had been heading north when first spotted about 9:30 a.m. turned around and headed south again. It seemed to be moving in a circle, coming closer as it turned, and, finally, at about 11:45 a.m., it headed out to sea to disappear over the horizon.

The ICO Barge and Boat Editor would welcome suggestions as to what the curious maneuvers mean. Could the ship of foreign registry have been fishing within our twelve mile limit? And if so, should we have reported it, and if so, to whom?

The ICO does not emphasize crime news. There's not a whole lot to emphasize anyway. Sometimes a young show-off will be caught driving ninety miles an hour along Highway 1. "Why give him any publicity?" Joanna asks. "That's all he wants anyway."

She does take a firm stand on political issues that affect the region. She was against the final legislation that kept the coast commissions in power. Most people who live here agree with her. It is not that they want unrestrained growth. Heaven forbid. But they believe they are better able to know what is needed than any distant, elite-minded and costly bureaucracy. More on that later.

On all controversial subjects, the paper tries to present both sides of the argument and has been commended for fairness many times. Its editorials are clearly labelled as such and they often make incisive statements you will rarely see in a large metropolitan paper or hear in a speech by a politician who wants to be elected.

The paper began publication in 1969 as a semi-monthly. It now has a circulation of eighteen hundred, comes out every week and can include as many as twenty tabloid pages. It has subscribers all over the West and in Germany, Holland, Scotland and the Netherlands.

When Joanna and her husband, John, a retired engineer, opened shop, "all our friends thought we were out of our minds." It wasn't a matter of making a newspaper man's dream of running a country weekly come true. Joanna had been out of the business for many years. "It just happened. We thought we would issue a small newsletter at The Sea Ranch, but the more we talked to people, the more we saw that there was a need for a regular paper. So here we are."

At first the ICO had to be printed in Ukiah. All the material was taken over at four o'clock in the morning so the work could be done while the big city presses were idle. In a few years, an offset press was purchased and installed in Gualala. Now John, the production manager, gets up at three o'clock to print, but he doesn't have to drive a hundred and eighty miles over the mountains.

Their son, J. Stephen, is the advertising manager and also a writer. The paper employs a layout artist, a typesetter, an equipment technician and another writer. They are all photographers.

Is anybody getting rich?

"Nobody," said Joanna with a laugh. "It's only been the last couple of years that my husband and I could draw small salaries. But it's fun."

The experience of Joanna and her family represents an ideal solution to the problem of survival on this coast . . . or anywhere else, for that matter. They live in an area they love; they have recognized one of its needs; they have been thoroughly successful in meeting it.

And so they have both economic and emotional fulfillment.

Not everybody is able to handle it as well. There just aren't too many opportunities, economically at least.

Making a buck isn't easy here.

WAYS TO IMPROVE
EACH SHINING HOUR

Those who escape to the South Seas often get bored after six months or so. "There's nothing to do except fish, make love and drink beer," is a common complaint.

"What's so bad about that?" is a common answer.

No one can truthfully say that the Mendocino coast is lacking in opportunities for any of the above activities. There are a few other possibilities, however, that seem to offer considerable enjoyment.

Let me list some.

Look but don't eat. The Amanita Muscaria.

Mushroom Roulette

Once the rains start and on through the winter, the woods are full of a wide variety of mushrooms and any number of pickers who play an exciting game. I may be overemphasizing its element of danger, but it does exist. For example:

One of the loveliest mushrooms you'll ever see is the *Amanita Muscaria*. It has a brilliant vermilion cap, maybe five inches across, flecked with white scales. Its stem and gills are soft, white and smooth enough to invite a caress.

But the *Amanita muscaria* is poisonous.

It is also called the "Fly Mushroom" because pieces of it were once put in saucers with water to kill flies.

The *Amanita rubescens* looks very much like it, except that the cap is reddish brown, the flecks a bit grayish, the stem pinkish and perhaps not quite so smooth. It is supposed to be edible, but, for heaven's sake, don't take my word for it.

102

Many of the *Bolateses* are delicious; others in the same family can make you ill.

The point is, you'd better know what you're doing before you fill your basket for pot or skillet.

Everyone has always admired the man who ate the first oyster. I would add the man who ate the first mushroom and his descendents over the years who have compiled the following warning notes.

Edible mushrooms usually have a pleasant smell, but this smell shouldn't be too strong. Those with an unpleasant or rancid smell are definitely bad. If the flesh is soft and watery or heavy and fibrous, discard. If the mushroom has an acrid, acid or peppery taste, stop eating. If it secretes a milky fluid that tarnishes pewter or a silver spoon or turns onions black . . . well, that's a good sign it's a bad sign. If the flesh of the mushroom changes color when cut, especially if it turns blue, toss it in the garbage can. Old poisonous mushrooms may have changed enough in the aging process to look like a safe species.

Now, if you still want to go mushrooming, fine. There are many people who have been doing it for years and haven't made a mistake . . . yet.

I must admit we've been a bit timid so far. We *have* gathered fresh Chantrelles which are distinctive in shape and color. Cooked slowly in a little chicken broth and thickened with cream, they're excellent.

I didn't intend to send you back to your local market for your mushrooms, but if I did, there's something else you can do with the fantastic fungi. Photograph them. They come in so many shapes, colors and configurations, they're a beautiful challenge. There are opportunities here few photographers in the world are lucky enough to have.

Wildflower-UP

This is another game best played with a camera, but, of course, it needn't be.

You start on square one knowing, as I did, that there are at least two

recognizable wildflowers: the poppy and the lupine. This gives you con-
fidence and a sense of purpose. You now have to find, recognize and
perhaps record about a hundred and fifty more. They're all here and
worth the search.

You can play the game any time of the year. There's always something in bloom. But it's best to start in January and February when the
most prolific season begins. You'll need a book, of course, preferably
with color shots. One by Dorothy King Young called, *Redwood Empire
Wildflower Jewels,* published by Naturgraf, is very good.

If you want to do the botany bit and learn scientific names, good
luck. I prefer the descriptive names. In fact, they're extremely helpful.
Once you've seen an "Indian Paintbrush," you won't forget it. A
"Yellow Monkeyflower" and a "Hairy Cat's Ear" soon become un-
mistakable. "Chinese Firecrackers," "Mission Bells," "Diogenes Lan-
tern," "Blue Eyed Grass" . . . well, you get the idea.

Some wildflowers grow near the sea, others in meadows, others in
the woods, others at high elevations, others in marshes. So if you play
the game, you tend to get around.

Many people get hooked, have special close-up lenses, even special
cameras, to record their finds. They're hard to compete with.

"Look," they announce smugly, "It's a Dwarf Brodiaea."

Your best answer: "It *is* a Dwarf Brodiaea. It certainly is!"

Since they're always right, you can't be wrong.

Still, I can now tell a Yellow Skunk Cabbage blossom when I see
one. I certainly can.

Variations of Same

This game can be expanded to include trees and bushes and grasses
that grow along the bluffs and in the meadows.

It doesn't take long to learn to recognize a redwood and know that
you haven't seen them all if you've seen one. Most of the giant, first-
growth trees are long since gone along this coast, but there are a lot of
second-growth groves in the valleys and along the hills where fog is
present during the summer.

The fog ghosting through the trees condenses on the needles and drips to the ground, providing moisture the magnificent trees seem to need to survive.

The Bishop pine (or Bull pine), with its clusters of long needles, is very common. It is one of the few species that grow right up to the bluffs along the ocean.

Enough? If it isn't, you can learn to know the western hemlock, the Monterey cypress, the Sitka spruce, the Douglas fir, the western yew, several willows, the wax myrtle, the tan oak, the red alder, the eucalyptus, the madrone, the manzanita, the Oregon ash and a number of others.

Tree and bush buffs recommend making a collection of pressed leaves carefully labeled. Why not?

The most colorful bushes are the rhododendron and the western azalea. They bloom in April and May and can be seen along the roads, beside streams and in the woods. It's a good time to drive with considerable caution. You can never tell when the car in front of you is going to come to a sudden halt.

There are few houses along the coast that don't have bouquets of dried grasses, and they're extremely attractive. Because of the salt spray that coats them, they dry to a golden yellow color, and they retain their shape for several years. The time to pick them, of course, is after they've dropped their seeds in the late spring and before they're battered by the summer winds. There are varieties here that are found nowhere else on earth.

You can play the game of label and catalog with grasses, too.

At the moment, knowing "Rattlesnake Grass" is my finest achievement in the field.

Driftwooding

Driftwood on the beaches is replenished each winter and redistributed by the storms. New stuff comes floating down the brown, flooding rivers in the rain; old stuff is washed out to sea, banged against the rocks by the waves and tossed ashore newly shaped. Piles of drift-

Watcher from the woods.   Photo by Julie Verran

What's more fun than dragging kelp?   Photo by Julie Verran

Small wave, small rock . . . pow!

An ancient beach, now rock-hard.

wood are often huge, and they are searched again and again all summer long. Somewhere in the jumble is the perfect piece for someone.

Perfection, I've discovered, is definitely in the eye of the beholder. What looks exciting to one person may look dull and commonplace to another. I've even seen this cause trouble.

Once I watched while a young husband held up piece after piece for his wife to see. The tenth time she said, "Yech," he growled, "Okay, find your own goddam driftwood," and stomped off down the beach.

I suppose a piece of driftwood *is* a work of art and deserves an emotional reaction. I'm afraid it all looks pretty good to me. I like to see it around. If I bring some home that isn't greeted with enthusiasm, I don't suffer much. I know I can always toss it on the fire and enjoy its blue and green sparks.

Beachcombing

On a ranking from one to ten, the Mendocino beaches would probably rate a bit below five when it comes to beachcombing. You don't find a wide variety of shells, for example, and most are broken by the waves and rocks. There are abalone shells, of course. They're pretty tough. Some enthusiasts search for different sizes and nest them from the largest to the smallest. There are also sand dollars. These are often attached to weathered boards and used as decorations. Scallop shells are fairly common, too.

Agates? Yes, they can be found from time to time. Once in a while a glass float will come bobbing in from Japan.

Doubloons? Well, the Spanish galleons used to sail right by on their way to Mexico from the Orient. If you're a dedicated beachcomber, you'll probably keep it in mind.

Birdwatching

For some peculiar reason I've always been fascinated by water, sea and shore birds and only mildly interested in land birds. Oh, I like watching Stellar's jays. They're feisty, peppery and tell the whole world off. Quails are enjoyable, especially when they herd their families around. Hawks hanging in the air are hard to ignore.

But I've never gone out into the woods, binoculars at the ready, to seek out a wrentit or a nuthatch.

In terms of sheer numbers, the Mendocino coast is not one of the world's best places to watch land birds anyway. More than four hundred species can be found in California. Only about a hundred visit this area, and many of these simply pass through in the spring or fall.

You'll find the turkey vulture here, however, a variety of hawks, owls, doves, swallows, thrushes, wrens, meadowlarks, sparrows, finches, blackbirds, warblers, phoebes and, once in a great while, that finest of all singers, the mockingbird.

I know I've missed a number on this brief list, but one more simply has to be added and with an exclamation point: the hummingbird. There are hundreds of them (Anna's, Rufous, Allen's) and they'll often leave their flowers on the deck, hover outside our windows and stare in.

Serious Thinking

The professor arrived at our door one day to explore an idea. He had taught political science for many years, his last school being San Francisco State.

"I have been thinking it might be interesting," he said, "if a few of us got together, say, once a month. The thought would be to take turns writing and reading a paper. We could all discuss it, kindly of course. If we could get a dozen people, it would mean we would each have to produce something once a year. That shouldn't be too much of a chore."

"A bunch of serious thinkers?"

He smiled. "In a way, yes."

"Writing a *paper* sounds . . . well, a bit difficult. Research, organization, conclusions, validations, writing. You're used to it. Are there enough people around who'd want to do that amount of work?"

"I think you might be surprised. A lot of knowledgeable people live in these woods. They should be encouraged to share their ideas, interests. And I hope it *will* be hard work, that we all strive for a considerable degree of excellence."

I agreed, a bit apprehensively I'll admit, that it was worth a try.

And so it was the Discus Club was soon formed. It started with ten members and has grown to fifteen who vary in age from their early forties to the seventies. They include the professor, of course, a couple of writers, the judge of the Point Arena court, a house designer, two retired chemists and another who is still consulting, an ex-marketing executive, a National Park Service man and some recent additions whose backgrounds I haven't pinned down.

Whoever reads a paper provides the house, beer and potato chips. The members arrive promptly at five and leave at seven. There's usually enough beer left to help the reader survive his ordeal.

Subjects? A surprising variety so far, and all covered extremely well. How Natural Laws Affect Codified Law, The Making of a General, How the Greek Gods Punished the Innocent, Holistic Medicine, Why Drake Couldn't Have Landed in San Francisco Bay, Diseases of Animals Transmitted to Humans, New Laws that Protect Consumers, Life in Australia, Producing Electricity with Magnetic Fields.

When my turn came, I struggled through a paper on Man's Greatest Stupidity, War.

They all listened attentively and with sympathy.

Tough subject. I'm not sure how convincing I was, but I was glad to get it all off my chest.

And I was ready to enjoy the three cans of beer they'd left.

Serious Painting

My friend, Charlie, a Scotsman from Australia, was utterly delighted the last time I saw him. He's been painting seriously for two or three years now, probably something he'd wanted to do all his life. He

110

and a group of other artists, mostly beginners, go on expeditions, bring a picnic lunch and have at it with the help of an instructor.

"She's marvelous," Charlie said. "Always looks for the good things in a painting. Never negative. She doesn't tell you what you've done wrong and inhibit the hell out of you. She finds what's good and helps you go from there."

But that wasn't the reason for Charlie's delight.

"We went up to this ranch back in the hills," he said, "and painted a big old barn. I really put the color on thick. Used a palette knife and slammed right into it. Turned out bloody good, I thought. But the best part is . . . the ranch owner liked the painting so much he bought it from me. Gave me a ham and half a lamb!"

IN THE BALANCE

It must be reasonably apparent by now that the Mendocino coast is a simple place to live and attractive to those who like simplicity.

There are not a whole lot of things to do.

Once you've seen the trees, the waves, the cliffs, the birds, the wildflowers, the sunsets, you look at them again. For a lot of us, that's plenty. For everybody? I'm not sure that sheer beauty is enough.

My wife is a part-time rental agent for houses on The Sea Ranch. One caller asked to rent a house for a week. More often than not rentals are just for weekends. In the middle of his call, he paused, and she could hear him shout to his wife "Are you *sure*? Seven full *days*? Don't you think we'll start going out of our minds?"

He was probably right to wonder.

It must be remembered that many of the ingredients that make mass tourism successful and high rise hotels rise higher are missing on this coast.

Our beaches may be ruggedly beautiful, but girls on them are usually more comfortable wearing down jackets than bikinis, and what fun is there in that? The ocean is cold and dangerous to swim in. Surfers say the waves rise too abruptly and come in too close together. Anyone who tries to water ski should have his head examined. There are very few little harbors where boats can be docked and the cocktail flag hauled up. Sailing is doggone hard work. There are only two nine-hole golf courses and very few tennis courts. We have no winter sports or gambling casinos.

The appeal of this coast is, I think, highly selective.

And yet it's hard not to wonder what it will be like in the future.

We all know about Carmel. Recently, on a weekday, more than fourteen thousand cars were counted on its main street. Its motels, and there must be hundreds of rooms available, were ablaze with "No Vacancy" signs.

I lived in Sausalito when it was a wonderful small village. The building where the *Trident* and *Ondine* restaurants now have long waiting lists for tables was a place that sold fishing bait. Sally Stanford's? Well, the ex-madam then had a much more interesting commodity to sell than food. Ernest Gann, soon to become a best-selling author, made his living fishing and selling his catch fresh off the boat. It was possible to amble along the street and not feel part of a parade. Except for a few bars and the movie, everything closed up by nine o'clock.

Maybe Carmel and Sausalito are better today than they were in the old days . . . more fun, more exciting. They certainly provide work for a lot of people, especially meter maids.

But how much progress is enough?

Will the Mendocino coast go that way too? There is already some evidence that it could. The town of Mendocino, with many of its old buildings restored and an enterprising arts and crafts colony hard at

114

Old railroad trestle weathered to an art form.

work, is crowded a good share of the summer. It's often difficult to find a parking place. Mendocino, of course, is reached by a much better road than that which serves the south coast. Highway 1, with its Jenner grade, is a deterrent that protects us somewhat . . . at least for now.

But what would happen if a new road were built. A four-laner through a pass in the mountains is not an impossibility. Then we'd be as close to San Francisco, in time as well as mileage, as Carmel is.

Many of us who live here and love the area do not fancy the prospect, but we don't believe all growth should be fought either. We cannot sit barking in our mangers simply because we got here early. As a matter of fact, considerable growth is needed, both for the benefit of those who are here and could use more jobs and those who visit and would like a reasonable variety of places to stay.

It seems to us that "simplicity" is the word to keep in mind when it comes to growth. What makes the region unique is that it is simple, remote, tranquil and naturally beautiful. If developers are allowed to have a field day and begin to provide all the things people can find other places, much of that appeal could be lost. On the other hand, if there is slow growth, carefully watched so that the character of the area is enhanced and not violently changed, it might be good for everyone.

This kind of speculation, of course, came to an abrupt end with the passage of the Coastal Initiative and later the Coastal Act of 1976. The decisions now are being made by two commissions.

Perhaps this is necessary.

Most old residents and the bright-eyed environmentalists from out of town are in fundamental agreement that the coast should definitely be protected from runaway exploitation. But all has not been peaches and cream.

For a number of people, commission decisions have caused considerable hardship. Even though they bought lots and paid taxes long before the Initiative and Coastal Act were voted on, they have not been able to build the single family homes they planned; they may never be able to; there is no evidence that they will ever be reimbursed. All they can do is sit and wait for their yearly tax bills.

This, for some reason, has been particularly true on The Sea Ranch, a development which has been in existence for more than a decade. Its concept was anything but short-sighted in terms of environmental values. On the contrary, The Sea Ranch planners were far ahead of their time, and the development won many awards for its sensitivity to the need for preservation and conservation. More than half of its total acreage was kept in commons that could not be touched. Houses were built in clusters. A style of architecture was insisted on that would blend into the landscape . . . natural wood exteriors that would weather, no paint, no fences, no eaves. Cars could not be visible. No non-indigenous vegetation was allowed. Trees were planted and meadows seeded with native grasses and wildflowers to help stop wind erosion, a real problem when sheep grazed on the land.

It was the kind of development a coastal commission might dream up itself and recommend as a model.

True, The Sea Ranch included 5,200 acres, but the total area to be covered by roads, driveways and roofs was less than ten percent.

Too large? Possibly. Possibly not.

Still, The Sea Ranch is simply not a Waikiki kind of development and was never intended to be. Yet it is being treated as if it were. And a lot of people have been caught in the middle.

Some of my best friends, to borrow the old saying, live or own lots on The Sea Ranch. They're really nice folks when you get to know them and probably as a group are more concerned with sound environmental practices than anyone you could name.

As one retired schoolteacher put it, "I won't even walk through a meadow for fear of stepping on a wildflower, and I've been made to feel I'm a criminal because I own a lot here."

What is even more puzzling is that many of the so-called protectors of the coast are outspoken in their insistence that the public be granted almost total access to it, even if it means forcing rights-of-way through people's property.

They might have a point if, as on a good share of the Atlantic coast, there were very little access. Actually, there is a tremendous amount. California established ten state parks between San Francisco and Fort Bragg many years ago. These include thousands of acres and many beaches where there are toilets and containers for beer cans and other trash if they are only used. Point Reyes National Seashore and, more recently, the Golden Gate National Recreation Area have added another hundred thousand acres. There are also a number of county parks and entrances through privately owned property.

There's a dichotomy here. If "protection" is the umbrella word, too many high-rises will not protect the coast, but neither will unrestrained access with brigades of visitors tromping across the fields and scrambling down cliffs six-packs at the ready.

117

It should be remembered that much of the coast does not have access, public or private, for a very good reason. It is simply too precipitous and dangerous. Any man who owned part of it would be a fool to grant access. How much insurance would he have to carry? Who'd clean up the potato chip bags and the empty bottles?

I once asked the leader of our local rescue squad what advice he would give a young family that wanted to hike along the bluffs and find some nice little secluded cove for a picnic.

He groaned. "I'd tell 'em to stay the hell away. We've had to pull too many people out of the water already, and they were awfully dead. There are plenty of safe places to go."

Shouldn't some of the beaches be left for the starfish, hermit crabs and blennies in their tidepools?

The politician who said, "The coast should be there for all twenty-two million Californians to enjoy," may know how to get votes, but he doesn't seem to care much about the delicate balance of the ocean's shore.

How it will all be settled is difficult to say.

It could be simple if it is kept simple.

But it probably won't be.

WHERE LESS IS MORE

Although the major purpose of this book is to describe what it is like to live on the rugged coast of Northern California, you may be wondering what it is like simply to visit.

So, for a chapter, let me play guide.

Whenever we've traveled, we've found that local knowledge is pretty reliable, and I'll try to give you as much as I have. Also, I should warn you that we like to seek out unusual places to stay and are perfectly willing to sacrifice some of the creature comforts you'll find behind the familiar signs that beckon from most major highways. Wall-to-wall carpeting, glasses wrapped in cellophane bags—even a private bathroom—are not essential if we can find an old hotel with character, an especially good view, a garden or an orchard to wander around in, a sense of privacy and, above all, a door that does not open on an acre of solid asphalt crammed with the noses of automobiles.

If you share this viewpoint, there's much to recommend a trip to the north Sonoma and Mendocino coast. It *is* different.

As the owner of one small cluster of forty-year-old cabins told me, "We don't have telephones, and our floors may creak and slant a bit, but we do have fireplaces, trees and decks where you can watch the ocean. People seem to like it."

Don't misunderstand me. Some of our accommodations are luxurious and will cost you a bundle. Some are simple and charming. Many have kitchen facilities. There are inns in turn-of-the-century houses that serve excellent food and have rooms furnished with antiques. There are a few standard motels. And there are a number of good restaurants. Three, at least, have been commended by *Gourmet* magazine.

There are also fine places to camp.

Of course, you can whip through from San Francisco and return in a single day, but I wouldn't recommend it. You'll see a lot of splendid scenery, but you'll be driving constantly.

If you can, come during the week. Weekends are often crowded, especially when they include holidays or happen to fall at a period of low tides during the abalone season. By crowded I don't mean bumper-to-bumper jammed, but it's a good idea to have a reservation if you want to stay someplace special. If you don't book ahead, you'll usually be able to find a good bed, however, and it's always possible to continue on to Fort Bragg where there are a number of motels.

Bring your woollies, as they say in England. Even if it is blistering in the interior valleys, it will be much cooler along the ocean. It can be windy and possibly foggy during the summer. Spring and fall days are usually bright, clean and warm, and winter days, between storms, can be magnificent.

Spring really starts late in January, and from then on through June is the best time to see the wildflowers.

By all means, pack a picnic kit.

Shopping? If you've read this far, you know that a lot of artists and craftsmen work here. The principal place to see their efforts is in the town of Mendocino, but there are others along the way. I'll try to point them out.

Routes to Take

The fastest way to get here from San Francisco is to drive up Highway 101 just past Santa Rosa to an exit marked "River Road" and turn west toward the ocean. This road follows the Russian River past vineyards (Korbel has a winery tour and a champagne tasting room), orchards and through redwoods. About fifteen miles beyond Guerneville it joins Highway 1 near the town of Jenner. Follow Highway 1 north. To this point, you will have driven about two hours, maybe slightly less.

If you choose to travel Highway 1 all the way, don't plan on making good time. The road has many curves. There are places you'll want to stop. You may want to try Tomales Bay oysters. They're large and not considered to be the world's choicest, but they're good in chowders and stews. Bodega Bay is a colorful fishing port. A restaurant called *The Tides* serves seafood fresh off the boats.

Many visitors enjoy leaving Highway 101 at Petaluma and taking the road to Bodega Bay that angles up through some strangely beautiful country. Rounded hills, very few trees, long vistas, graceful old barns, dairy herds. On this route you'll join Highway 1 just a few miles before you reach Bodega Bay.

In any case, all roads lead to Jenner, for that is where you begin this particular journey.

The Start is Dramatic

I've mentioned the Jenner grade, and you'll recognize it when you leave town and begin to drive up the hills along the ocean. Be of good cheer. The difficult part lasts only about fifteen minutes. Here you will see an unusual sight in America: sheep grazing along the road and sometimes crossing in front of you. This is an open range. So be careful, but don't be too concerned. Sheep are smarter than they're said to be.

121

On clear days you can see miles down the coast, a view that would be world-famous if it were in Europe.

Following are places where you may want to stop. They are listed in the order you will reach them as you drive north.

Fort Ross Historic Park

When the Russians were coming, this is where they came. In 1812, ninety-five of them, along with forty Aleut and Kodiak Indians, arrived from Alaska, built a fort, a church and about fifty buildings, including a large tannery and a boat construction shop. One of their reasons for choosing the spot was an abundance of sea otters with marvelous fur pelts. The otters were hunted in kayaks by the skilled Alaskans who sometimes took as many as a thousand a day. When the lovely little animals had all but disappeared, the Russians pulled up stakes and went home. Their stay ended in 1841.

Fort Ross is now a state park and is well worth a visit. The stockade, church and blockhouses have been reconstructed, and one of the original buildings, the Commandant's House, has been carefully restored. There are trails along the bluffs, spectacular scenery and a pleasant picnic area.

Timber Cove Lodge

A dramatic, heavily timbered structure that confronts the sea and the winds as if it were there to stay. You'll also recognize it by a tall, slender, colorful column that stands just outside. This is Beniamino Bufano's statue, "Peace," topped by a hand raised in blessing. The lodge has rooms that look out at the sea, a bar and a restaurant.

Ocean Cove Motel

A standard motel, but one with fine views. Its small restaurant is much better than you might expect and is reasonable in price.

Stillwater Cove Regional Park

One of Sonoma County's newest public parks with a sheltered cove divers like to use. It covers sixty acres and includes a beautiful redwood grove with a creek. It's a nice place to picnic. There are no campsites at the moment, but some are planned, and they should be ready soon.

Stillwater Cove Ranch

If you can remember struggling to stay awake in a schoolroom, it may please you now to sleep in one to your heart's content. The ranch was once a boys' school, and its buildings have been converted into a hotel. The rooms are large, comfortable, and all but one have fireplaces. You can also rent what was once the cow barn which has sleeping bunks for eight. Some of the rooms have kitchen facilities, but no restaurant operates except by special arrangement for groups. The grounds are spacious and full of trees.

Salt Point State Park

One of the newest and most rewarding parks in the state system. Salt Point has an exceedingly beautiful stretch of coastline. It also has miles of hiking and riding trails through forests and grasslands. Nearby is Kruse Rhododendron State Reserve where you can stalk the wild, pink flower in its natural state. The best time is May. There are picnic areas and a campground.

Stewarts Point Store

It was originally built in 1868 and still looks much like it did early in the century. Well worth a stop.

The Sea Ranch

The Sea Ranch Lodge, I think, deserves to be highly recommended. Its rooms are large and colorfully decorated. Some have fireplaces. It has a good restaurant, and its cocktail lounge looks out across the meadows to the sea. Guests have the use of a protected swimming pool and tennis courts. A nine-hole golf course is available at reduced rates. Room prices are lowered during the winter.

You can also rent private homes or condominiums for a two-night minimum or longer. These are architecturally exciting with all modern facilities included except bed linens. Some are luxurious. Many have won design awards. Usually, the houses sleep from four to eight people, and often two or more couples gang up and share expenses. Children are welcome.

Gualala Point Regional Park

Another of Sonoma County's new public parks and a fine one. It includes a long, broad beach that closes the mouth of the Gualala River all summer long. Lots of driftwood. There are also bluffs where you can watch for whales and often, in late April and May, see them very close to shore. There's a picnic area and a campground.

Gualala River Redwood Park

A privately owned camping area on the north side of the river about a mile east of Highway 1. The campsites are located in a large grove of redwoods. The weather is warmer than it is by the ocean, and you can swim in the river if the water is high enough. If not, splash around anyway.

Gualala Hotel

The big white building dominates the town as it has since 1903 when it was a stagecoach stop. It's a friendly, relaxed place with a big barroom that really jumps on Saturday nights. The Gualala Hotel restaurant serves very good meals with an Italian emphasis, including an hors d'oeuvre tray, family-style soup tureen, a variety of entrees and a daily special. The room is charmingly old-fashioned and much favored by the locals. Prices are reasonable.

If you're adventurous, you can get a room at the hotel which hasn't changed much since logging days. Some steelhead fishermen have stayed here for years and wouldn't go anyplace else. But be prepared to share a bathroom down the hall and hear laughter in the corridors at any hour of the night. It's probably not the place to spend your honeymoon. Then again, who knows?

The Surf Motel

We used to stay here often. It's not the newest motel you've ever seen, but it's clean, comfortable and reasonable in price. Some units have kitchens.

Need Provisions?

The Surf Super Market is a well-stocked store with just about anything you may need, including a new pair of Levi's.

The Old World Deli has a wide selection of cheeses, cold cuts, prepared salads, beers and wines. The owners also make huge sandwiches to go, saving you the trouble.

The Big G is a drive-in where you can eat on a sunny deck or carry away a bag for your picnic. Good place for kids.

The Sea Lion

A restaurant that offers home-cooked meals and very good sandwiches. Good value. Lots of truckers stop here.

The Dolphin

This is the shop run by Gualala Arts to showcase and sell the work of coast artists and craftsmen. It's located just behind the post office.

125

You'll find most anything from crocheted afghans to wood carvings, water colors to abalone jewelry. There are often times when artists are present to demonstrate how they work.

The Ark

An attractive small gallery at the north end of town just across from the mobile home park. It offers paintings, prints, photographs, plants and pottery, much of it from the area. It also has a fine selection of potted succulents.

St. Orres

I've already described this two-towered building at some length. It is now operating as an inn. There are eight bedrooms, each with specially designed redwood walls, built-in furniture and colorful handmade quilts. Bathrooms are shared down the hall, but they're very nice ones. Room rates include breakfast.

Its restaurant is excellent and dining under one of the towers with its stained glass windows is an experience in itself. St. Orres is open for dinner every night of the week and for luncheons Saturdays and Sundays.

Serenisea

About a mile or less beyond St. Orres is a cluster of cottages on a wooded bluff. Look sharp. The entrance, on the ocean side of Highway 1, is easy to miss. Currently, three units are rentable at very reasonable prices. Each has a fireplace, electric heat, a fully equipped kitchen, one or two bedrooms and a bathroom. They're charmingly furnished with bright, colorful rugs and other artistic touches. There are fine views of the ocean, a trail to a small beach and a tethered goat to keep you company.

Anchor Bay

A colorful little town that enjoys the best weather on the coast. It has a large general store, and its restaurant, Rusty Anchor, serves very good food at reasonable prices. It has an adjoining bar.

Anchor Bay Campground

Just north of town. Campers and trailers seem to use it more than tenters. It's located on one of the warmest beaches you'll find, and you can launch a boat there if you have one handy.

Mar Vista

Called a "motel," but it really isn't one at all in the present-day sense. Mar Vista is a collection of twelve one and two-bedroom cottages spread around a duck pond. All have kitchens. If you're old enough to remember, they'll remind you of places you stayed in the thirties and early forties, for that is when they were built. Some have been modernized . . . that is, carpeted and fireplaced. The view down the coast is lovely. Beach access is just across the road down a long flight of wooden stairs worth descending even if you may puff a bit coming up.

The Sea Urchin

A pleasant gallery, one of the first in the area. Paintings, pottery, driftwood artifacts are for sale. Also, a good selection of nature books to help you know the coast better and big, white sweaters knitted by hand in Greece.

Point Arena

This is the area's big town, with two motels and a number of restaurants, stores, a movie and even a bowling alley. Nobody's ever tried to make Point Arena anything more than it is for years. It has its own special charm.

Whistling Swans

You may be able to see one of the rare sights on earth just after you leave Point Arena and begin to descend into the Garcia River valley. Whistling swans winter here, and there aren't too many of them around anymore.

Manchester State Park

So you want to walk or jog on a lonely beach? There's one here that will give you all the scope you could ask for. Picnicking, camping.

Elk Cove Inn

One test of a good inn is how long it stays open under the same management. This one has been owned and operated by two young people, Roger and Hildrun-Ute Noteware, since 1967 and has a loyal following. Their home, an old Victorian on a bluff just as you enter town, is the restaurant. The hotel is in another building about half a mile away. Hildrun-Ute cooks continental dinners, German food more often than not. Roger plays Bach on the piano to heighten your enjoyment. The inn is open for from twelve to fourteen guests on Fridays, Saturdays and Sundays. Room price includes both breakfast and dinner.

Greenwood Pier Restaurant

Simple and pleasant. The food is good, cooked by people who like organically grown vegetables and believe that alfalfa sprouts are here to stay.

Harbor House

A splendid old redwood building built in 1916 with very attractive rooms. There are also some cottages. The Harbor House outdoor terrace is alive with hummingbirds and is one of the loveliest places on the coast to watch the ocean and study a profusion of sea stacks. Fine beach and exceptional food. Often full weekends, so call ahead. Price includes both breakfast and dinner.

Gregory's

A small restaurant on an ocean bluff just before you reach the Albion bridge. Its reputation among the locals is excellent, and even they are pleased with the view.

The Andiron

An unusual motel in that its units are scattered in a number of buildings around spacious grounds, so you get some privacy. Each has a fireplace, kitchen equipment and a deck.

S.S. Seafoam Lodge

Another fine motel, also a cut above the ordinary. No kitchens, but there are outstanding views from floor-to-ceiling windows and decks.

Heritage House

Certainly a queen of quiet country inns. The Dennens, who run it, were among the first to restore an old State of Maine style house and open it to the public for food and lodging. They've done an admirable job, and the inn has grown almost every year. Now most of the rooms are in separate buildings among the trees. There are paths, beaches, bluffs, cliffs and, of course, the ocean. Flowers are everywhere. It's the only place around where gentlemen are requested to wear neckties and jackets to dinner. Breakfast and dinner (both highly acclaimed) are included in the price.

Schoolhouse Creek Inn

Cabins and units are rustic but comfortable with nice views and fireplaces. Some are being refurbished, part of an on-going project by new and very friendly owners. One of the outstanding restaurants on the north coast is on the same property.

The Ledford House

Owner and Chef Barbara Mastin cooks like an angel and miraculously turns out dinners, each to order, for as many as fifty guests a night. Her soups, salads, homemade brioches and desserts are excellent. Usually, she offers a choice of three entrees, including one local fish. Her fresh salmon, thick steaks oven-poached and served with a lively sauce, is about as good as it can be. Her shrimp cannelloni is worth the trip. Plan on an unhurried meal. Mrs. Mastin's personal attention takes a little time.

Van Damme State Park

A beach, of course, but you should also explore its Fern Canyon where millions of the plants can be seen. A Pigmy Forest is a short drive up the airport road just south of the park entrance. Here full-grown cypress and pine trees stand at heights of from six inches to five feet.

Little River Inn

Again you'll see the influence New England had on the early settlers.

The Little River Inn is a rambling white building with porches that looks very much like old hotels on the Atlantic. It now has some new cottages and motel-like units, giving visitors a wider choice of accommodations than they'll usually find. There's a bar and a good restaurant where the abalone is recommended. You can also play golf on a nine-hole course.

Mendocino

Twenty-five years ago, I was transferred by my company from San Francisco to New York. We weren't exactly overjoyed. We started our long journey east by poking along up Highway 1 and got only as far as Mendocino the first night. We were delighted when we figured out that we'd made no progress at all. A whole day's driving, and we were farther away from New York than we were when we started!

The town was fascinating then, and it is even more so now. A remarkable job of restoration has been done. The old Victorian houses which once sagged sadly, paint peeling, steps rotting, have been beautifully rebuilt. The village looks fresher and more appealing every time we visit it, as we now do fairly often.

It could well be the high spot of your trip, so plan to spend some time there if you can.

It would be difficult to report individually on all the places you should see. There are now at least forty shops, most specializing in one or another form of art and craftwork. They're located in an area only a few blocks square, so it will be easy to walk around and make your own discoveries.

I will mention Zacha's Bay Window Gallery on Main Street, not only because it features the work of Mendocino's Art Center faculty, but because its proprietor was one of the prime movers in all the restoration efforts. The Kelly House, now a museum, should be on your list, too.

It's fun to stay overnight in Mendocino, and you can find rooms unlike any you may have seen before at several places.

The Mendocino Hotel has been enlarged and is now much more elegant than it ever was in its long history. There's an abundance of

"Long John Sliver" in Anchor Bay.

There'll be fresh salmon tonight.

Photo by Julie Verran

Artists think big in Mendocino.

Farms look much like they did early in the century.

Photo by Julie Verran

Barn in silhouette reveals its graceful lines.

Photo by Julie Verran

A north coast supermarket. Well, almost.

133

stained glass, much lovely dark wood paneling. The bedrooms are bright and sparkling with large old-fashioned beds. If you stay in a room that doesn't have a bath, you'll be given a robe to wear walking down the hall. It has a good restaurant and bar.

MacCallum House was once one of the town's famous mansions. It is now an extremely attractive old inn where there are said to be ghosts — very happy ones, you'll be assured. It has its own restaurant and small bar. You can have breakfast brought to your room if you choose. It always includes a heaping bowl of fresh fruit.

Mendocino Village Inn is another converted Victorian house with prices somewhat lower than the others. It does not serve food. Some of its rooms have fireplaces and private bathrooms.

As for restaurants, there are not too many, but the variety is interesting. One specializes in homemade soups. There's a deli that also serves sandwiches, salads, imported beers and wines. The Foghorn promises entertainment with dinner.

Cafe Beaujolais has a well-deserved reputation for its gourmet cooking and recently has begun to offer a special dinner during the week at a price that pleases the locals. We've always enjoyed eating at The Seagull which is reasonable and popular. Incidentally, The Seagull also has rooms that might be worth checking out.

For Sea Food Buffs

Just before you reach Fort Bragg, you'll cross a bridge and see the entrance to the Noyo fishing harbor. It's a busy one, especially during the salmon season.

If you're staying somewhere that has cooking facilities, you may want to visit the Noyo markets. There is not a tremendous selection of locally caught fish, but what there is — especially the salmon — is very good. If you can find sanddabs or rex sole, you're in luck. These delicate little fish (which should be cooked simply in butter and not too

Sea caves are to explore.   Photo by Julie Verran

135

long) are two of the real treats on the Pacific coast. Lingcod, red snapper and rock cod are usually to be had. They're heavier in texture. Once in a great while cabazone fillets are available. We always get more than we can eat, poach it all and save the leftovers for a salad the next day. You could easily mistake it for crab.

Crab? You'll find it here during the season, but most of it is caught near Eureka. Does that make any difference? Not really.

Abalone? If it's available at all, it was probably taken near Monterey or even Mexico, frozen and shipped in. To be at its very best, abalone should be absolutely fresh. Try to make a lot of new friends quickly. One of them may invite you to dinner.

Well.

Our little trip has covered roughly a hundred miles. I hope I have made it clear that most of your pleasures will be simple ones.

Still, being able to walk on a deserted beach, poke through piles of driftwood, watch the pounding surf, picnic in a meadow full of wildflowers or enjoy the peace of a redwood grove is not to be dismissed too lightly.

They're rare opportunities these days.

LADIES BY THE SEA

Book jacket covers of a good many Gothic romances show the heroine in a hooded cloak walking toward a somber stone house on a bluff above the ocean. The sky is dark and foreboding. Grass whips in the wind. Waves crash against the rocks. There may be one tiny light in the house or, better still, none at all.

What is she doing out on such a stormy evening? Why is she going to that scary place? What evil lurks there?

We can guess, of course, almost with certainty, that she's a young girl from the city (let's call her Chrissie) who has been hired to be the governess of two small children. Her employer, a handsome, enigmatic man whose wife died suddenly, has not met her, as he had promised, at the station. There is no place to stay; she knows no one; she has decided to walk to her new home before the rain sets in.

Brave girl.

I asked my wife, "Why is it so many women think living by the ocean is romantic? It's often the scene of novels. Does it make your heart go pitty-pat?"

I told her about Chrissie.

She laughed and said, "Your Chrissie is interesting because she's in a dangerous situation, not necessarily a romantic one. A woman can identify with her, but not really want to be in her shoes. In most of those books, remember, it takes the heroine a long time to begin to like being by the sea. She spends a lot of terrified nights listening to the wind howl and the shutters clap."

"Did it take you a long time to get to like it?"

"Me? You know that's a silly question. I've always loved the ocean, the stormier the better. But I know many women don't want to be too close to it. They'd rather live up in the hills or maybe a half mile away with a distant view of it. On The Sea Ranch, for example, a good share of the houses are built where the ocean can't be seen at all . . . and that's true of Gualala, too."

"My mother, for example? She didn't like it at all."

"She certainly didn't."

I'll never forget her comment after looking out the window for quite a while. "Look," she said, "you know I want to be cremated when I die. But don't you *ever* scatter my ashes on the ocean."

So it goes.

"Well," I persisted, "forgetting about that for the moment, is this a good place for a woman . . . whether she lives in a pine grove or on a rock, two feet above high tide?"

"It is for me," she said quickly, "but I'm not sure it would be for every woman."

"What do you mean?"

"Well, it isn't a place to be pretty and feminine, to have . . . oh, the center of a stage."

138

"I thought that was rapidly going out of style."

"Not entirely. To a lot of women it's still important to be on display, to whirl around with their friends in a social scene, dress up in the newest clothes, be with it. That doesn't happen much here. Who dresses up? And why should they? It just isn't practical."

"You mean you miss that sort of thing?"

"Not in the least, but some women would. They might also miss a country club, for example, where there was something doing all the time. Or going to art exhibit openings, the theatre, seeing the latest movies, trying new restaurants. Or shopping."

"There's always the Pay n' Take," I reminded her.

"That's hardly I. Magnin. These things can be important. Not much to me anymore, once in a while, though. That's why some of the women who came up here found it too hard to adjust and insisted on moving back. They didn't realize how much they'd miss all the opportunities of the city and the suburbs."

"Big letdown, huh?"

She nodded.

"But most of the women we know seem able to handle it, don't they?" I asked.

"Of course, but they're all pretty self-sufficient, have things they like to do . . . knitting, weaving, painting, writing. They all use their time. And oh . . . there's something else I think is extremely important."

"Yes?"

"I believe that any woman who moves here should be certain of one thing . . . that she and her partner, husband or otherwise, are very good friends. They could both be lonely if they weren't."

"Okay, friend," I said. "Put on your prettiest dress and I'll play you a game of Scrabble."

I imagine her last observation is true no matter where a couple goes to begin an alternative lifestyle. They'd better have the battle of the sexes settled before they try the great adventure. Any drastic change

Chrissie's observation post.

requires adjustments. Values simply have to alter, and it is not often easy to discard old ones. I would say it's impossible if one partner is lukewarm and goes along reluctantly. Both better have an upbeat attitude.

I do not want to leave you in suspense about Chrissie. She arrived at our door just after the rain started on Christmas day, looking wet and miserable but not the least bit terrified. She was no bigger than my hand, and she waited with one paw raised until we let her in.

She told us off for not meeting her, ate heartily and was soon purring in front of the fire.

No problems of adjustment whatsoever, and, except for one unpleasant visit to the veterinarian, she has lived a happy, if unromantic, life ever since.

THE YEAR'S
BEGINNING

During the long summer, the wind blows from the northwest along the coast raising whitecaps but very little surf. Suddenly, early in October, there comes a day when the flow of the ocean changes. A deviaton to the west. Although the sea is still visually placid, the sky clear of clouds, an occasional swell appears, hardly discernable until a hundred yards from shore when it gathers force, becomes a wave and crashes against the cliffs. Spray climbs high in the air; there is a *harrumph* that hasn't been heard in months; the earth shakes.

A sea cave just below the house has been hit like a drum dead center.

This does not mean that a storm is imminent. It means that the great Pacific High has weakened and the jet stream has begun to carve its way south. We may read of rain in Washington and Oregon, but here the sun is bright and hot, the ocean blue all the way to the curved horizon.

How long? Not long at all.

In a few days, perhaps a week, thin clouds begin to appear, high cirrus that do not threaten but hang like practice brush strokes in the sky and turn peach color as the sun descends. Good to see. It's been a long time since there was a proper sunset. During the summer, the sun seems to pause a moment above the fog bank then plunges in, becoming a misshapen orange ball in a kind of belly dancer undulation. A spectacular moment, but only a moment.

Tonight the colors linger and intensify for almost an hour. There will be rain before morning.

This time has always been the year's beginning for me, and it is more so now than ever before. Living on the ocean, it is impossible not to be acutely aware of the parade of seasons and the stream of life that surrounds us. The migrations of birds, the coming and going of seals and whales, the blooming and fading of flowers are constant reminders.

For all our ego, is it really possible that we are special creatures . . . apart from the rest?

It hardly seems possible.

We breathe, hold our heads up for a few short years, love, strut and fret (strut a little, fret a lot) and soon are replaced.

Can there be more than this?

I have not found the answer and am content to search no longer.

The clouds on the horizon are now completely gray. The rocks lift their huge shoulders out of the water (to borrow again from Jeffers). Gulls glide by in silhouette.

It is good to be here.

That is enough.

Roger Verran worked as a writer, creative director and vice president for one of the world's big advertising agencies, Batten, Barton, Durstine & Osborn, in big cities—Minneapolis, San Francisco and New York. Now he writes books, articles and edits a magazine in Gualala, California, a town so small you can drive through it in about one minute. But, he notes contentedly, it's right next to a big ocean.